● 英语翻译核心课程系列 ●

LIAISON INTERPRETING

联络口译

■ 王斌华 伍志伟 编著

武汉大学出版社

翻译考试资格必备·英语翻译核心课程系列

编 委 会 名 单

余　东　教授（广东外语外贸大学高级翻译学院）
莫爱屏　教授（广东外语外贸大学高级翻译学院）
张保红　教授（广东外语外贸大学高级翻译学院）
王斌华　副教授（广东外语外贸大学高级翻译学院）
刘军平　教授（武汉大学外语学院）
汪　涛　副教授（武汉大学外语学院）
严志军　副教授（南京师范大学外语学院翻译系）
陈剑芬　老师（西安外国语大学高级翻译学院）
刘建珠　副教授（深圳职业技术学院应用外语系）
黄建凤　教授（广西大学外国语学院）

前 言

按照国际惯例，口译可分为"会议口译"（包括交替传译和同声传译）和"联络口译"两大类。联络口译是一种由同一译员在同一场合中担任两种语言方向（如英译汉和汉译英）口译的工作模式，又称"对话口译"、"社区口译"、"公共服务口译"。联络口译是一种最常用的口译形式，广泛应用于外交会晤、商务会谈、外宾陪同、旅游导览、参观访问、法律服务、医疗服务等各种场合。

本书是国内最早专门训练联络口译技能的教材。本书缘起于2008年6月武汉大学出版社外语事业部编审谢群英女士的约稿。当时她问我，现在口译学生最缺的是什么教材？我当即告诉她，口译学生最缺的是一本"联络口译"的教材。作为一名口译教学一线的教师和口译实践一线的译员，我注意到，一方面联络口译是一种应用范围最广泛的口译形式，另一方面联络口译也是外语专业学生初入职场时最容易找到的工作机会，但目前国内外均无专门训练联络口译的教材。听完我的回答和解释，谢编辑当即决定，约请我编写出版这样一本专门面向联络口译的教材。

虽然我们的想法很好，但要实践起来谈何容易！由于没有先例可循，本书从编写理念的形成到编写大纲的设计以及编写内容的组织都颇费思量。经过仔细调研和认真探索，我们决定把本书设计成一本专门训练联络口译技能的教材。

本书的编写理念为：以联络口译的基本技能和典型场景为设计主线，以真实的工作案例为主要内容，以任务教学法的方式进行口译教学。每一章均设计成联络口译现场工作的一个方面的任务，围绕任务来进行联络口译技能、口译练习、口译表达等方面的教学设计，让学生在模拟现场的教学环境中掌握联络口译的技巧，并熟悉联络口译各类典型的工作场合。

本书的整体设计如下：

全书内容共有15章，按"联络口译技能"和"联络口译场景"两条主线同时展开，各章之间按照由易到难的顺序编排。

联络口译技能主线为：联络口译导论、接待礼仪、导游口译、宴请口译、展会口译、谈判口译、商务礼仪、购物口译、送客礼仪、国际合作、文化差异处理、体育口译、政治外交口译、医疗服务口译、法律服务口译等。

联络口译场景主线为：外宾接待、旅游导览、宴请饮食、参展参会、商务洽谈、参观访问、在中国购物、送客道别、教育合作、文化交流、体育活动、政治访问、中医中药、法律事务等。

各章内容设计如下：

1. 联络口译技巧（Liaison Interpreting Tips）：结合本单元的联络口译任务，扼要讲解联络口译技巧，介绍该工作场合的相关知识，如语言、文化和交际知识等。这部分内容可在课前由学生预习或在课堂由教师扼要讲解。

2. 口译任务准备（Task-based Preparation）：准备本单元口译主题相关的常用词汇表达（Useful Expressions）和口译套句（Interpreting Formulas）。本部分内容可在课前预习。

3. 联络口译练习（Liaison Interpreting Practice）：围绕口译主题展开的若干场联络口译。本部分练习书后附有参考答案，供学生参考使用。这部分内容宜在课堂进行仿真训练。

Ⅳ. 口译难点讲解（Notes for Interpreting）：分点讲解本单元口译中的难点。可根据学生的具体情况进行讲解或留待学生课后复习。

本书适合作为翻译专业的口译课入门教材和英语专业的口译课核心教材，对于有志于从事联络口译工作的英语学习者以及参加"人事部翻译资格（水平）考试"和上海市"外事联络陪同口译水平认证考试"的考生，本书也适合用作进行系统自学的教材。

本书编写者是两位口译教学和实践一线的教师。王斌华设计编写理念和各章内容，编写其中九章，伍志伟编写其中六章，最后由王斌华统稿修订。

在编写本书的过程中，我们广泛参考了各种与联络口译和外事外交有关的文献资料，主要有：外交部、广东省人民政府外事办公室、北京市人民政府外事办公室的官方网站，中国2010年上海世博会官方网站，广州开发区网站，国内各大旅游景点网站等，在此谨向有关方面致谢！

联络口译教材的编写在国内外都是一种探索，笔者经验有限。如有不足之处，敬请方家不吝指正。

编著者

2010年1月

目录
CONTENTS

Chapter 1　Introduction to Liaison Interpreting　联络口译导论 …………… 1

Chapter 2　Etiquette of Receiving Guests　接待礼仪
　　　　　口译主题：外宾接待 ……………………………………………… 7

Chapter 3　Tour Guiding　导游口译
　　　　　口译主题：旅游导览 ……………………………………………… 12

Chapter 4　Dining & Cuisine　宴请口译
　　　　　口译主题：宴请饮食 ……………………………………………… 21

Chapter 5　Exhibitions & Fairs　展会口译
　　　　　口译主题：参展参会 ……………………………………………… 32

Chapter 6　Business Negotiations　谈判口译
　　　　　口译主题：商务洽谈 ……………………………………………… 40

Chapter 7　Business Etiquette　商务礼仪
　　　　　口译主题：参观访问 ……………………………………………… 47

Chapter 8　Shopping in China　购物口译
　　　　　口译主题：在中国购物 …………………………………………… 57

Chapter 9　Seeing Guests Off　送客礼仪
　　　　　口译主题：送客道别 ……………………………………………… 62

Chapter 10　Cooperation Talks　国际合作
　　　　　 口译主题：教育合作 ……………………………………………… 66

Chapter 11　Dealing with Cultural Differences　文化差异处理
　　　　　 口译主题：文化交流 ……………………………………………… 76

Chapter 12　Sports Interpreting　体育口译
　　　　　 口译主题：体育活动 ……………………………………………… 85

Chapter 13   **Diplomatic Interpreting**   政治外交口译
                 口译主题：政治访问 ……………………………………………… 94

Chapter 14   **Medical Service Interpreting**   医疗服务口译
                 口译主题：中医中药 ……………………………………………… 106

Chapter 15   **Legal Service Interpreting**   法律服务口译
                 口译主题：法律事务 ……………………………………………… 116

Answers for Reference   口译练习参考答案 ……………………………… 126

Chapter 1　Introduction to Liaison Interpreting
　　　　　　　联络口译导论

Ⅰ. Liaison Interpreting Tips

Do you want a career as an interpreter? Are you fluent in two languages? Perhaps you are already working or volunteering as an interpreter and want to improve your professional skills. This course provides you with fundamental professional skills in the field of liaison interpreting.

To gain the professional knowledge and skills in Liaison Interpreting, to learn to perform interpreting tasks using accurate language and register, to develop your vocabulary for various interpreting situations, to gain an understanding of how to manage the ethical dilemmas interpreters may face, and learn to employ effective and appropriate cross-cultural skills for your work as a liaison interpreter in China, you must learn this course, which gives you an understanding of the nature and practice of liaison interpreting.

After this course, business, community and government agencies can be sure that you have the necessary knowledge and skills to work effectively and professionally as a liaison interpreter in a wide range of settings.

1. Interpreting vs. Translation

In order to define interpreting in general, it is useful to relate it to another activity with which it is often confused, i.e. translation. The two activities are similar in that they both involve the understanding of the source language and of the underlying meaning, but they are different in terms of the process used to transfer and deliver the message in the target language. In most cases, translation involves written texts and therefore the translator has the opportunity of revising and improving the previous version of the translation. Unlike translators, interpreters have to deal with fleeting messages which

they have to convey orally under time constraints, with very little room for error repair or stylistic improvement.

2. Liaison Interpreting as a Type of Interpreting

As far as types of interpreting are concerned, the main distinction is made between **conference interpreting** and **liaison interpreting**.

Conference Interpreting

Most people would have some understanding of what is meant by conference interpreting. There are two sub-types within this category, based on the interpreting mode used by the interpreter: **simultaneous interpreting**, which occurs virtually at the same time as the original discourse, and **consecutive interpreting**, which, as its name suggests, follows a segment of speech varying in length from one short statement to an entire speech:

- **Simultaneous Interpreting** is the most common form used for multilingual meetings and a major mode of interpreting for international conferences, in which interpreters work in sound-proof booths in teams of two per language combination, listening to the speaker via headsets and taking turns in simultaneously delivering the translation via microphones straight into the headsets of their audience.

Benefits: no time lapse, most professional interpreting mode. Smoothest choice for listeners.

Requirements: professional simultaneous interpreting skills, simultaneous interpreting equipment including booths, central units, headsets, sound system.

- **Consecutive Interpreting**, on the other hand, is most often used for single speeches and requires the interpreter to take notes before giving the interpreting at appropriate intervals or at the end of the speech.

Advantage: It does not require any technical equipment except for microphones.
Disadvantage: It requires almost as much time as the source-language presentation, i.e. the time involved almost doubles.

Liaison Interpreting

Liaison Interpreting is a generic name for the type of interpreting performed in two

Chapter 1　Introduction to Liaison Interpreting 联络口译导论

language directions by the same interpreter.

Unlike conference interpreting, liaison is more personalized interpreting service where the provider mediates a conversation by interpreting messages in multiple (usually two) language directions, i. e. both from English to Chinese and from Chinese to English. Liaison interpreting is best suited for more informal meetings between a smaller number of people, or perhaps as an escort for someone visiting a country whose language they do not speak. When using the services of a liaison interpreter, speakers usually pause after every one to two sentences so that the interpreter (who usually listens attentively without taking notes) can deliver the interpreting.

It may also be called Dialogue Interpreting or Three-cornered Interpreting (e. g. in Australia), Community Interpreting (e. g. in Scandinavian countries), Public Service Interpreting (e. g. in the UK), Bilateral Interpreting, Ad Hoc Interpreting and Cultural Interpreting.

Liaison interpreting tends to be used in less formal situations where there are many natural breaks in conversation for the interpreter to speak. Consecutive interpreting is used in more formal situations where the speaker deliberately pauses after slightly longer sections (e. g. paragraphs) of a speech for the interpreter to speak.

It is probably the most common form of interpreting activity today, given that it takes place in varied settings in which the interpreter—working between two languages—is usually physically present, mediates between two or more individuals who do not speak each other's language and usually uses the consecutive mode of interpreting.

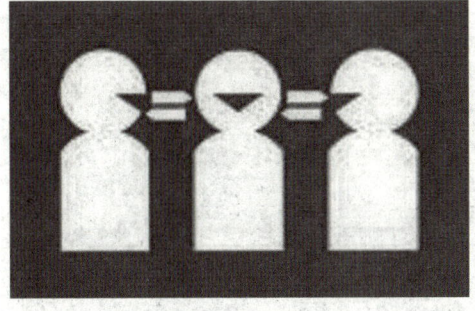

Liaison Interpreting

3. Working Mode of Liaison Interpreting

In some occasions of liaison interpreting, the interpreter escorts the interlocutors or the small delegation; in some other occasions, the interpreter and the interlocutors sit together at a table or a working lunch. The typical working mode is that the interpreter translates a few sentences at a time. When the speaker has finished, the interlocutor responds and again the interpreter translates. Therefore the liaison interpreter interprets in both language directions.

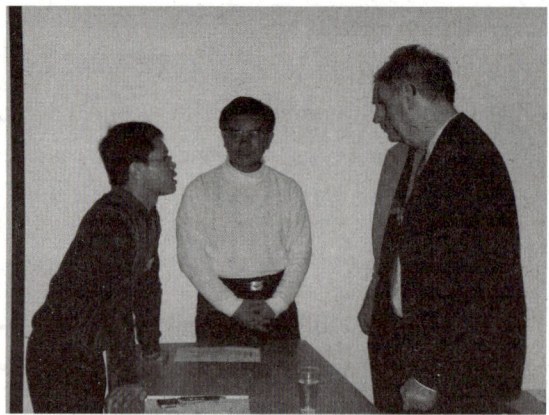

Working Mode of Liaison Interpreting

4. Liaison Interpreter

The liaison interpreter provides—usually short consecutive—interpreting between two languages in both directions. The liaison interpreter is often required in job assignments

Liaison Interpreter (the man on the left)

to accompany an individual or delegation around. Liaison interpreters usually intervene to facilitate legal consultation, guest relations, and business or diplomatic meetings. They are always affiliated to the host company and act as facilitator in negotiations or undertake some public relation activities.

5. Settings and Fields of Use of Liaison Interpreting

The settings in which liaison interpreting is used include various general professional environments such as business and diplomatic negotiations and meetings, sight-seeing tours and education or cultural contacts, as well as many public services situations in which people who are not fluent speakers of the official language(s) of the country where they reside have to communicate with the providers of public services, i.e. in legal, health, education, government and social services settings.

6. Group Liaison Interpreting

Group Liaison Interpreting is a type of consecutive face-to-face interpreting used where a small group of people requires an interpreter. Although called "group liaison" this type of interpreting can also include situations where individual group members need an interpreter.

Group Liaison Interpreting is commonly used for groups for which conference interpreting would not be appropriate because the group is too small, or needs to move around (meaning interpreting booths are impractical) or simply because the group does not want the formal approach that conference interpreting gives.

This kind of interpreting works well in situations such as:
- a guided tour of business premises
- tourist groups
- groups visiting tourist attractions
- a small group attending a presentation or being addressed by a speaker
- corporate hospitality events

Group Liaison Interpreting is also a very flexible interpreting arrangement. We realize that many visits or events have a number of different components to them. A typical day might involve many different elements:
- a group presentation
- a question and answer session
- lunch

- a tour of premises
- one-to-one conversations
- dinner or a social event

With Group Liaison Interpreting, the interpreter moves with the group from one part of the day to another and is on hand throughout to interpret and help group members.

7. Qualities Required of a Liaison Interpreter

Three "Pillars" of Interpreting Competence

- Bilingual competence: Bilingual competence is one of the foundations building up an interpreter. A liaison interpreter must be proficient in both of the working languages, esp. in listening comprehension and oral expression.
- Extra-linguistic knowledge: Extra-linguistic knowledge is the other foundation building up an interpreter. As a liaison interpreter working in various settings and in different fields, one must "know something about everything", i.e. to have a wide encyclopedic knowledge and subject knowledge.
- Interpreting skills: Interpreting skills, including skills in listening comprehension short-term memory, transference and reformulation and expression, are the core of interpreting competence. Professional training or systematic learning is required in order to master interpreting skills.

Other Qualities Required of a Liaison Interpreter

- Psycho-physiological qualities (e.g. ability to concentrate, outstanding memory, pleasant voice, quick-wittedness, calm nerves, insatiable curiosity in new things & ideas)
- Cross-cultural awareness
- Strong sense of responsibility and good professional ethics

II. Liaison Interpreting Practice

Role Play 1

Please work in groups of two, playing the roles of a foreign guest visiting your university and an escort liaison interpreter.

Role Play 2

Please work in groups of three, playing the roles of a liaison interpreter and a small delegation visiting your city.

Chapter 2 Etiquette of Receiving Guests
接待礼仪
口译主题：外宾接待

I. Liaison Interpreting Tips

Making introductions is always the first thing that a liaison interpreter needs to do while receiving foreign guests. **Mastering the art of introductions is a must for a liaison interpreter.** Every day we encounter people in a variety of business and social situations. The way we meet and greet them creates lasting impressions and paves the way for a productive encounter. Introductions project information. Besides the obvious elements of name, title and professional affiliation, an introduction conveys a level of respect and reflects how the person making the introduction views the other persons' status.

The most important point about introductions is to make them. Failing to do so causes embarrassment and discomfort. If given a choice, most people would prefer you to make the introduction incorrectly, even if you forgot their name, rather than stand there unacknowledged and disregarded.

A second important point in any introduction is the order of names. The name of the person being introduced is mentioned last, and the person to whom the introduction is made is mentioned first. The rules for who is introduced to whom depends on whether it's a business or a social introduction.

Business Introductions: In business, introductions are based on power and hierarchy. Simply, persons of lesser authority are introduced to persons of greater authority. Gender plays no role in business etiquette; nor does it affect the order of introductions.

For example, you would say, "Mr./Ms. Greater Authority, I would like to introduce

Mr./Ms. Lesser Authority." However, the person holding the highest rank may not be Mr./Ms. Greater Authority. A client, for instance, always takes precedence over anyone in your organization, as does an elected official.

Social Introductions: According to rules of international diplomatic protocol, people are presented to royalty, chiefs of state, ministers in charge of legations, ambassadors and dignitaries of the church regardless of age or gender. The woman's or the man's name would be mentioned last and the distinguished person is mentioned first.

But, there are the exceptions to the rule. Social etiquette is based on chivalry, so both formal and informal introductions are made according to age, then gender, and then social status. The man would be introduced to the woman in a social situation unless the man is obviously a great deal older, in which case one would defer to age over gender. For example, if both persons are of the same generation, you would say, "Mrs. Jameson, I'd like to introduce Mr. Horton." But, if the woman is considerably younger, you would say, "Mr. Horton, this is my daughter Hilary."

As you make the introduction, include a brief but meaningful piece of information about each of the people to explain their uniqueness or importance. "Sally is the PR consultant who helped me get all that coverage in the national press. Bob is the photographer whose work you admired in my office, Sally."

Responding to Introductions: The way you respond to someone else's introduction is just as important as making the introduction. In response to informal introductions, simply say "hello". Add a phrase like, "I've heard so much about you, Barry," only if it is true and if it is complimentary.

"How do you do?" followed by the person's name is the customary response to a formal introduction. Refrain from the use of first names until the person to whom you've been introduced has indicated that the familiarity is preferred.

II. Task-based Preparation

1. Useful Expressions

airliner 班机   airsick 晕机

Chapter 2　Etiquette of Receiving Guests 接待礼仪

international flight　国际航班
domestic flight　国内航班
boarding gate　登机口
boarding pass　登机牌
check in　登机（手续）
departure time　起飞时间
arrival lobby　入境旅客休息室
information　问讯处

main lobby　大厅
declare　（行李）申报
luggage; baggage　行李
hand-luggage　手提行李
luggage check　行李票
fellow traveler　旅伴
off season　旅游淡季
on season　旅游旺季

2. Interpreting Formulas

［1］请问，您是从……来的……吗？Excuse me, are you... from...?
［2］欢迎来到广州！Welcome to Guangzhou!
［3］这是您的第一次中国之旅吗？Is this your first trip to China?
［4］我敢肯定您在这里会有一个美好的旅行。I'm sure you will have a nice trip here.
［5］好久不见了！Haven't seen you for ages!
［6］最近还好吧？How have you been doing?
［7］祝您在这儿旅行愉快！Hope you enjoy your stay here!
［8］旅途愉快吗？Did you have a nice trip?
［9］坐飞机感觉如何？How was your flight?
［10］这么长时间的旅行，您是否觉得有点累了？Do you feel tired after the long trip?
［11］你习惯时差了吗？Are you adjusted to the time difference?
［12］我们城市的变化很大。Great changes have taken place in our city.
［13］正在变得越来越繁荣。It's becoming more and more prosperous.
［14］我在……宾馆为您预定好了房间。I have made a reservation for you at...
［15］我们将在……时间内到达宾馆。We will arrive at the hotel in...
［16］请填好这张入住登记表。Please fill in the registration form.
［17］请向他们出示您的护照。Please show them your passport.

Ⅲ. Liaison Interpreting Practice

Dialogue 1
Scenario：*Greetings and Introductions*

1.1

A：请问，您是来自美国的杰克逊先生吗？

B: Yes.
A: 很高兴见到您,杰克逊先生。我是中国旅行社的王维恩。欢迎来到广州。
B: Nice to meet you, Wayne. It's very kind of you to come and meet me.
A: 我很荣幸。我是您在中国期间的导游和翻译。
B: OK. Thank you.

1.2

A: 您好,杰克逊先生。好久不见。
B: Hello, Wayne. Yes. Last time when I saw you in Shanghai was three years ago.
A: 最近一切可好?
B: Pretty well. How about you?
A: 还好。祝您这次在广州旅行愉快。
B: I'm sure I will.

Dialogue 2

Scenario: *Asking about the Trip*

2.1

A: 旅途愉快吗?
B: Yes, it was wonderful.
A: 哦,那好。对于坐飞机旅行,这样最好了,你说呢?
B: Sure it is.

2.2

A: 这么长时间的旅行,您是否觉得有点累了?
B: Yes, a little. But I'm more excited.
A: 那晚饭前先到宾馆休息一会儿如何?
B: OK.

Chapter 2　Etiquette of Receiving Guests　接待礼仪

Dialogue 3

Scenario：*On the Way to the Hotel*

A：这是您第一次到中国吗？
B：Yes. All things are new to me.
A：中国是个美丽的国家，我敢肯定，您在这儿一定会旅行愉快。
B：I hope so.
A：您对这个城市第一印象如何？
B：I'm rather impressed by the prosperity of the city.
A：是的，我们城市的变化很大，正在变得越来越繁荣。
B：I enjoy seeing such a colorful and energetic city.
A：对了，我在白天鹅宾馆为您预定了房间。
B：OK, thank you. When can we reach there? I'm looking forward to setting in.
A：半小时内就能到宾馆。
B：That would be nice.

Dialogue 4

Scenario：*Checking in at the Hotel*

A：好的，我们到了。我们到前台办理入住登记吧。
B：Since you have made the reservation, what shall I do next?
A：请填好这张入住登记表就可以了。
B：OK. Shall I show them my passport?
A：是的，他们得确认您的护照号码。
B：OK. Here you are.

Ⅳ. Notes for Interpreting

中国人迎接远道而来的客人时，往往会说："您一定很累了吧？"但如果直译，对于来自西方的游客，他们并不一定能体会这句话本来的关切含义，甚至会误以为你怀疑他的体力。所以，翻译时应注意运用英语中该场合的适当问候语。作为联络口译译员，我们应该注意：英语和汉语的对应往往不是体现在字面上的，中西方文化的差异也很值得注意，我们要做到的是跨语言和跨文化的沟通。

— 11 —

Chapter 3　Tour Guiding　导游口译

口译主题：旅游导览

Ⅰ. Liaison Interpreting Tips

As a liaison interpreter of tour guiding, your priority is to make the guest(s) interested in the tour and comfortable during the tour. On the way to tourist sites, you can introduce background information about the site or talk on subjects that may interest him/her. You can also discuss the schedule. During the visit on-site, always make yourself helpful to your guests and try your best to render accurate and rich information for him/her.

Ⅱ. Task-based Preparation

1. Useful Expressions

中国国家旅游局　China National Tourism Administration
中国国际旅行社总社　China International Travel Service
中国旅行社总社　China Travel Service
旅游管理局　tourist administration bureau
旅行社　travel service/agency
旅游公司　tourism company
团体旅游　group/party tour
包价旅游　package tour
春/秋游　spring/autumn outing
假日旅行　vacation tour
蜜月旅行　bridal/honeymoon tour

持证导游　licensed tourist guide
导游译员　guide interpreter
实习导游　student guide
自然景观　natural scenery/attraction
人文景观　places of historic figures and cultural heritage
旅游景点　tourist attraction/sight/destination; scenic spot
山水风光　scenery with mountains and rivers; landscape
名山大川　famous mountains and great rivers
名胜古迹　scenic spots and historical

Chapter 3　Tour Guiding 导游口译

sites
避暑胜地　summer resort
度假胜地　holiday resort
避暑山庄　mountain resort
蜜月度假胜地　honeymoon resort
国家公园　national park
古建筑群　ancient architectural complex
洞穴/岩洞　cave; cavern
溶洞　water-eroded cave
石灰岩洞　limestone cave
石笋　stalagmite
钟乳石　stalactite
瀑布　waterfall; cascade
温泉　hot spring
陵墓　mausoleum; tomb
古墓　ancient tomb
石窟　grotto
祭坛　altar
楼　tower; mansion
台　terrace
亭阁　pavilion
塔　pagoda; tower
廊　corridor
石舫　stone boat
堤　causeway
湖心亭　mid-lake pavilion
水榭　waterside pavilion/house
莲花池　lotus pond
曲径　winding path
城堡　castle
寺庙/教堂　church
天主教大教堂　cathedral
修道院　abbey; cloister; monastery
尼姑庵　Buddhist nunnery
佛教圣地　Buddhist sacred land

琉璃瓦　glazed tile
宫殿　palace; hall; chamber
皇城　imperial city
护城河　moat
御花园　imperial garden
行宫　temporary imperial palace for a short stay
皇太后　empress dowager
皇妃　imperial concubine
宰相　prime minister
太监　court eunuch
四大金刚　the Four Guardians
十八罗汉　the Eighteen Disciples of the Buddha
出土文物　unearthed cultural relics
甲骨文　inscription on oracle bones
青铜器　bronze ware
景泰蓝　cloisonne; enamel
青瓷　celadon
陶瓷　ceramics
陶器　earthenware; crockery; pottery
瓷釉/珐琅　enamel
泥塑　clay figurine
折扇　folding fan
檀香扇　sandal wood fan
古玩店　antique/curio shop
手工艺品　artifact; handicrafts
木/竹/贝雕　wood/bamboo/shell carving
黄杨木制品　boxwood product
藤条制品　wickerwork
雕漆器　carved lacquer ware
刺绣品　embroidery
苏绣　Suzhou embroidery
挂毯　tapestry
唐三彩　trio-colored glazed pottery of the

13

Tang Dynasty
金石印章　metal and stone seals
字画卷轴　scroll of calligraphy and painting
国画　traditional Chinese painting
山水画/水墨画　landscape/ink painting
文房四宝　the four stationery treasures of the Chinese study including a writing brush, an ink stick, an ink stone and paper
保存完好　well-preserved
工艺精湛　exquisite workmanship
独具匠心　original/ingenious design
湖光山色　landscape of lakes and hills
景色如画　picturesque views
景色诱人　inviting views
湖石假山　lakeside rocks and rockeries
青山绿水　green hills and clear waters
园林建筑　garden architecture
佛教名山　famous Buddhist mountain

天下第一泉　the finest spring under heaven
上海的豫园、玉佛寺、外滩　The Yuyuan Garden, The Jade Buddha Temple, The Bund in Shanghai
北京的长城、十三陵　The Great Wall, The Ming Tombs in Beijing
北京的颐和园、天坛、故宫　The Summer Palace, The Temple of Heaven, The Palace Museum in Beijing
西安的大雁塔、碑林、古城墙　The Greater Wild Goose Pagoda, The Forest of Steles, The Old City Wall in Xi'an
西安的兵马俑、华清池、半坡遗址　The Terra-cotta Warriors, The Huaqing Pool Hot Spring, The Banpo Ruins of Civilization in Xi'an
桂林的叠彩山、七星岩　Piled Festoon Hill, Seven Star Cave in Guilin

2. Interpreting Formulas

[1] 上有天堂，下有苏杭。 In heaven there is the paradise, and on earth there are Suzhou and Hangzhou. / As there is the paradise in heaven, so there are Suzhou and Hangzhou on earth.

[2] 五岳归来不看山，黄山归来不看岳。 Trips to China's five great mountains render trips to other mountains unnecessary, and a trip to Huangshan renders trips to the five great mountains unnecessary.

[3] 黄山以"四绝"闻名，即：奇松、怪石、云海、温泉。 The Yellow Mountain is famous for its Four Wonders—fantastic pines, grotesque rocks, the sea of clouds and hot springs.

[4] 杭州四季气候宜人、风景如画，素有"人间天堂"的美誉。 Known as a Paradise on Earth, Hangzhou enjoys pleasant climate and picturesque landscape.

[5] 这十景是：苏堤春晓、平湖秋月、花港观鱼、柳浪闻莺、双峰插云、三潭印月、雷峰夕照、南屏晚钟、曲院风荷、断桥残雪。 They are Spring at the Su

Chapter 3　Tour Guiding 导游口译

Causeway, Autumn Moon over the Calm Lake, Viewing Fish at Flower Harbor, Listening to Orioles in the Willows, Twin Peaks Piercing to the Clouds, Three Pools Mirroring the Moon, Sunset View of Leifeng Tower, Evening Bell of the Southern Screen, Lotus in the Breeze at Crooked Courtyard, and Remaining Snow on the Broken Bridge.

[6] 来北京长城是必游之处，就像是到埃及必游金字塔一样。 The Great Wall is a must-see spot in Beijing, just like the pyramids in Egypt.

[7] 关于登长城，中国有一句家喻户晓的谚语："不到长城非好汉。" There is a popular Chinese saying about ascending the Wall. It goes, "If one fails to climb to the top of the Great Wall, he is not a true man."

[8] 苏州园林大概有150座，有些有1 000多年的历史。这些园林规模不大，但设计巧妙，它们寓诗人之神思、融画师之妙想，集自然美、建筑美和绘画美于一体。 There're about 150 gardens in Suzhou. Some of them are more than 1,000 years old. These gardens are not large but curious in their designs, and their designs are based on inspiration of poets and imagination of painters. They bring together the beauties of nature, architecture and painting.

[9] 今天我们将游览最著名的几处园林：狮子林园、拙政园、留园、网师园。 Today we will visit the most famous ones: the Lion Grove Garden, the Humble Administrator Garden, the Lingering Garden, the Master of Nets Garden.

[10] 中国画融合了诗歌、书法、篆刻等多种艺术的精华。 Chinese painting has incorporated the best of many forms of art, like poetry, calligraphy and seal engraving.

[11] 中国画根据版式可以分为以下五种：壁画、屏画、卷轴、画簿和扇绘。 Chinese paintings can be divided into five categories according to the format: murals, screens, scrolls, and albums and fans.

[12] 中国画的主题有人物、风景、建筑和花卉等。 The subjects of Chinese paintings include figures, landscapes, buildings, and flowers.

[13] 在中国文化中，松、竹、梅的形象是人们正直性格和良好品行的象征。 In Chinese culture, pines, bamboo and plum are meant to embody the qualities of people who are upright and show good moral behavior.

[14] 画上的题字和印章不仅可以帮助我们了解作画人的意图，而且还能增添装饰美感。 The inscriptions and seals on the paintings not only can help us understand the painter's ideas and emotions, but also add decorative beauty.

[15] 鉴定"美玉"的标准包括：硬度大、色彩柔和、感觉光滑、敲击的声音悦耳动听。 Standards used to gauge the value of jade are hardness, mellow color,

smoothness and pleasant sound.

[16] 玉器的特点是外形美观、线条流畅、图案复杂。 Characteristics of jade are elaborate and beautiful patterns, fluent lines and complicated images.

[17] 在中国文化中，打制玉器不仅是出于艺术方面的考虑，而且还因为玉的神秘意义和作用。 The jade pieces in Chinese culture are made not only for the sake of art; they also have mysterious meanings and functions.

[18] 在春秋时期，人们就把美德比作纯玉，玉的坚硬象征着坚定和忠诚，其光泽象征着纯洁和美好。 In the Spring and Autumn Period, people compared human virtues to pure jade. Its hardness suggested firmness and loyalty, and its luster projected purity and beauty.

[19] 我给你些旅游小册子看看吧。 Let me give you some brochures to look over.

[20] 今天我们去观光上海的市容吧。 Today we'll have a sightseeing tour round Shanghai.

[21] 这样的话，我建议您打的，或者坐观光巴士。 In that case I suggest you call a cab, or take a sightseeing coach.

III. Liaison Interpreting Practice

Dialogue 1

Scenario: *Visiting Natural Scenic Spots* 自然景观游

1.1 The Four Wonders of the Yellow Mountain 黄山四绝

A: 黄山以其"四绝"著称：奇松、怪石、云海、温泉。

B: Is the hot spring water here drinkable?

A: 可以。这里的温泉来自紫云峰，常年保持在42℃。泉水清澈，无色、无味、无毒。

B: Look at the clouds! The clouds and mists really look like a sea and ripples on the surface of the sea. The peaks look like islets in the sea.

A: 是的。您看这些松树。左手边是狮石和迎客松，张开怀抱像是欢迎登山游客。右手边是象石和送客松，枝叶招展犹如作别下山游客。

B: So many great attractions and so many wonderful sceneries on the mountain! It's really worth seeing.

Chapter 3　Tour Guiding 导游口译

1.2　Hangzhou and the West Lake　杭州西湖

A：杭州素有"人间天堂"的美誉。这里气候宜人、风景如画。杭州之美美在西湖。

B：It is said that the West Lake offers ten fabulous sceneries. What are they?

A：哦，西湖十景包括：苏堤春晓、平湖秋月、花港观鱼、柳浪闻莺、双峰插云、三潭印月、雷峰夕照、南屏晚钟、曲院风荷、断桥残雪。

B：Can we cover all of them today?

A：恐怕不行，但是可以看到大多数。

Dialogue 2
Scenario：*Visiting Historic Sites*　名胜古迹游

2.1　The Great Wall　万里长城

A：万里长城是北京之游必到的景点，就像埃及的金字塔一样。

B：I heard it's known as one of the wonders of the world.

A：是的，长城贯穿华北，全长 6 350 公里，合 12 700 华里，故称"万里长城"。

B：That's very impressive!

A：您知道吗？关于登长城，中国有一句家喻户晓的谚语："不到长城非好汉。"

B：So we're all true men now on the Great Wall!

2.2　Gardens in Suzhou 苏州园林

A：苏州的城市历史有 2 500 年之久，此地以园林著称。

B：What is unique of these gardens?

A：苏州园林大概有 150 座，有些有 1 000 多年的历史。这些园林规模不大，但设计巧妙，它们寓诗人之神思、融画师之妙想，集自然美、建筑美和绘画美于一体。

B：That sounds tempting. Today I would like to take a special trip of gardens in Suzhou.

A：好的，今天我们将游览最著名的几处园林：狮子林园、拙政园、留园、网师园。

— 17 —

联络口译

Dialogue 3

Scenario：*Enjoying Chinese Culture* 　中国传统文化游

3.1　Chinese Paintings　中国画

A：Look at these paintings. They're marvelous!

B：是的，中国画融合了诗歌、书法、篆刻等多种艺术的精华。

A：What lovely bamboo! Why do Chinese people like to draw pines, bamboo and plum?

B：在中国文化中，松、竹、梅的形象是人们正直性格和良好品行的象征，因此成为中国画的常见主题。

A：There is an inscription in this painting. What's the use of it?

B：画上的题字和印章不仅可以帮助我们了解作画人的意图，而且还能增添装饰美感。

A：Though Chinese paintings have much in common with western paintings from an aesthetic point of view, it still possesses a unique national character, right?

B：是的，中国画根据版式可以分为以下五种：壁画、屏画、卷轴、画簿和扇绘。

A：What about the subjects?

B：中国画的主题包括人物、风景、建筑和花卉等。

A：I heard one of the greatest master painters in China is Qi Baishi. Is that right?

B：是的，齐白石集赋诗、作画、书法和篆刻艺术于一身，是20世纪的艺术大家。

3.2　Other Works of Art　其他艺术品

A：How do you Chinese appraise jade?

B：品鉴"美玉"的标准包括：硬度大、色彩柔和、感觉光滑、敲击的声音悦耳动听。

A：Is jade precious?

B：当然，人们甚至认为玉器有某种超自然的神秘力量。玉器的特点是外形美观、线条流畅、图案复杂。

A：Why do people make ornamental jade?

B：嗯，在中国文化中，打制玉器不仅是出于艺术方面的考虑，而且还因为玉的神秘意义和作用。

Chapter 3　Tour Guiding 导游口译

A: What meanings and functions? Could you tell some?
B: 好的。古人相信，玉可以使灵魂不朽、使遗体不腐。在春秋时期，人们就把美德比作纯玉，玉的坚硬象征着坚定和忠诚，其光泽象征着纯洁和美好。

Dialogue 4
Scenario: *Touring the City*　城市观光游

4.1　Asking for Tourist Information　询问旅游信息

A: This is my first trip to Guangzhou, and I'd like to see some of the city's sights.
B: 广州有很多景点，最有名的包括：白云山、越秀公园、中山纪念堂、陈家祠和南越王墓。
A: Do you have some information on these?
B: 我给你一些景点小册子看看吧。
A: I'm curious about the Chen Clan Academy. Could you tell me more about it?
B: 当然可以。陈家祠是广东最大的宗祠书院之一，也是岭南建筑装饰艺术的代表。

4.2　Sightseeing tour of the city　市容观光

A: Today I would like to have a sightseeing tour round Shanghai. I'd like to visit the famous spots.
B: 好主意。上海最有名的景点有豫园、玉佛寺、外滩等。
A: Oh, I can't wait to go. But I've got only one day, so how can I visit all these places within a single day?
B: 那样的话，我建议您打的或者坐观光巴士。

Ⅳ. Notes for Interpreting

[1] 左手边是狮石和迎客松，张开怀抱像是欢迎登山游客。右手边是象石和送客松，枝叶招展犹如作别下山游客。
　　[译文]　On the left are the Lion Rock and Welcoming Pine which has stretched its boughs to welcome tourists up the mountain. On the right are the Elephant Rock and Farewell Pine which has extended its branches to bid farewell to tourists down the

mountain.

［2］这些园林规模不大，但设计巧妙，它们寓诗人之神思、融画师之妙想，集自然美、建筑美和绘画美于一体。

［译文］ These gardens are not large but curious in their designs, and their designs are based on inspiration of poets and imagination of painters. They bring together the beauties of nature, architecture and painting.

Note：中文导游词很注重措辞的美感，如句1中的"枝叶招展犹如作别"，句2中的"寓诗人之神思、融画师之妙想"即是典型例子。口译现场时间有限，即时口译的压力很大，译员无法像在笔译中那样可以"旬月踟蹰"，有充分的时间进行措辞的琢磨。因此，在口译现场遇上这类表达时宜采取意译为主的方式，抓住其中的关键词，并注意理解其意义，"神思"、"妙想"意义均为"想象"，口译重点在于表达句子的实质信息和意义。

Chapter 4　Dining & Cuisine　宴请口译
口译主题：宴请饮食

Ⅰ. Liaison Interpreting Tips

Table Manners

Table Manners in Western Countries
These apply to America and most of Europe. If you're elsewhere, do some research beforehand.

When men and women are eating together, men should pull out the chairs for women and see that all the ladies are seated before taking their own places.

The fork goes on the left. The spoon and knife go on the right. Food items go on the left, so your bread plate is on your left. Drinks, including coffee cups, should be on the right.

When sitting at a banquet table, you may begin eating when two people to your left and right are served. If you haven't been served, but most of your table has, encourage others to start. Reach only for items in front of you, ask that other items be passed by a neighbor. Offer to the left; pass to the right, although once things start being passed, go with the flow.

The Menu
Under no circumstances would a private dinner in the West, no matter how formal, consist of more than:

　　1. Hors d'oeuvre (appetizer)

2. Soup
3. Fish
4. Entrée（main course）
5. Roast
6. Salad
7. Dessert
8. Coffee

The menu for an informal dinner would leave out the entrée, and possibly either the hors d'oeuvre or the soup.

Filling Glasses and Proposing Toasts
As soon as the guests are seated and the first course put in front of them, the butler or the host goes from guest to guest on the right-hand side of each, and asks "Champagne?" or "Do you care for some wine or soda water, sir/madam?" and fills the goblet accordingly.

In China, it becomes accustomed that the host should keep proposing toasts to the guests to his/her hospitality and the host should always dry up his/her glass wine to show respect. In international communication settings, however, proposing toasts is appreciated but drying up the wine is not necessary.

II. Task-based Preparation

1. Useful Expressions

A. Chinese Food Menu　中餐菜单

1) Poultry　禽类

香酥鸡	Crisp fried chicken	陈皮鸡	Chicken with orange peel
北京酱鸭	Diced chicken with Beijing sauce	炒鸡丁	Stir-fried chicken dices
		栗子鸡	Stewed chicken with chestnuts
		盐水鸭	Salted duck
虾油鸡	Chicken with shrimp sauce	拌鸭掌	Cold duck webs
咖喱鸡	Curry chicken	北京烤鸭	Roast Beijing Duck
白片鸡	Chicken slices	南京板鸭	Steamed Nanjing duck cutlets

Chapter 4　Dining & Cuisine 宴请口译

酱爆鸭片　Sliced duck with bean sauce
八宝炖全鸭　Stewed whole duck with stuffing
脆皮火鹅　Crisp roast goose
卤鹅翼掌　Spicy goose wings and webs
炒乳鸽　Fried pigeon with lettuce

2) Beef and lamb　牛羊肉类
咖喱牛肉　Curry beef
麻辣牛肉丝　Shredded beef with hot pepper
姜丝牛柳　Ginger beef
五香牛肉　Spiced beef
羊肉串　Roast lamb brochettes
烤羊排　Roast lamb chops
葱爆羊肉　Quick-fried lamb with scallion in ginger sauce
清蒸羊肉　Steamed lamb
清炖羊肉　Stewed lamb in clear soup

3) Pork　猪肉类
糖醋排骨　Sweet and sour pork ribs
叉烧肉　Barbecued pork
软炸里脊　Soft-fried pork fillet
木须肉　Stir-fried pork with scrambled eggs
青椒肉丝　Sliced pork with green pepper
鱼香肉丝　Julienne pork in pepper sauce
炒腰花　Stir-fried kidney slices
蒜泥白肉　pork slices with mashed garlic
红焖肘子　Braised pork joint in red sauce
鲜菇肉片　Sliced pork with fresh mushrooms
锅巴肉片　Sliced pork with sizzling rice

4) Seafood　海鲜类
腰果虾仁　Stir-fried shrimps with cashew nuts
油焖大虾　Prawns braised in oil
虾仁豆腐　Shrimps with bean curd
广式龙虾　Cantonese lobster
红烧海参　Braised sea cucumbers with brown sauce
鲍鱼海参　Abalone and sea cucumbers
干贝鱼翅　Shark's fin with scallops
醉蟹　Wine preserved crab
姜汁大肉蟹　Fresh crab with ginger sauce
糖醋鳜鱼　Sweet and sour Mandarin fish
炒鳝片　Fried eel slices
清蒸甲鱼　Steamed turtle
干烧鱼块　Fish pieces with chili sauce
咖喱鱿鱼　Curry squid

5) Vegetables　蔬菜类
素什锦　Mixed vegetables
鱼香茄子　Eggplant with garlic sauce
辣黄瓜条　Cucumber slices with chili
干煸四季豆　Fried string beans
西芹百合　Stir-fried celery with lily

6) Soups　汤类
酸辣汤　Hot and sour soup
番茄牛肉汤　Tomato and beef soup
火腿冬瓜汤　Ham and melon soup
豆腐蛋花汤　Bean curd and egg drop soup
三鲜汤　Three delicacy soup
肉片汤　Soup with meat slices
西红柿蛋汤　Tomato-egg soup

B. Western Food Menu   西餐菜单

1) Cold dishes and appetizers   冷盘和开胃食品
Ham and sausages   火腿和香肠
Pickles   酸黄瓜
Smoked perch   熏鲈鱼
Pork jelly   肉冻
Bacon   咸肉
Liver paste   肝泥
Caviare   鱼子酱

2) Soups   汤类
Creamed mushroom   奶油口蘑汤
Creamed tomato   奶油番茄汤
Creamed asparagus   奶油芦笋汤
Chicken and noodle   鸡面清汤
Fish chowder   鱼蛤什锦汤
Ham and bean   火腿青豆汤
Vegetable puree   蔬菜浓汤

3) Entrée   主菜
Baked fish with butter   奶油烤鱼
Baked ham roll   烤卷筒火腿
Baked chicken with mushroom   口蘑烤鸡
Barbecued beef ribs   烧烤牛排
Beef steak with onion   洋葱牛排
Beef steak curried   咖喱牛肉
Broiled lobster with butter sauce   奶油扒龙虾
Broiled lamb chops   扒羊排
Fried mutton slices   炸羊肉片
Grilled veal   铁扒小牛肉
Roast chicken   烤鸡
Roast turkey   烤火鸡
Roast lamb leg   烤羊腿
Smoked pork loin   熏猪腰
Stewed beef   烩牛肉

4) Side dishes   附加菜
Asparagus with cream sauce   奶油芦笋
French fries   炸土豆条
Fried onion rings   炸洋葱圈
Fruit salad   水果色拉
Meat salad   肉色拉
Potato chips   炸土豆片
Seafood salad   海鲜色拉
Sweet corn with cream sauce   奶油玉米

5) Bread and cereals   面包和谷类食品
Bread   面包
Bun   (小) 圆面包
Cereals   早餐谷物制品
Corn flakes   玉米片
Doughnut   面包圈
Loaf   长面包
Oatmeal   燕麦片/粥
Pancake   锅饼
Toast   吐司, 烤面包

6) Fast food   快餐食品
Ham sandwich   火腿三明治
Fish fillet sandwich   鱼片三明治
Chicken sandwich   鸡肉三明治
Turkey club   火鸡肉三层三明治
BLT   咸肉生菜西红柿三明治
Hot dog   热狗
Hamburger   汉堡包

Chapter 4　Dining & Cuisine 宴请口译

Big Mac　麦当劳巨无霸
Mac chicken　麦香鸡
Cheese burger　奶酪汉堡

Double cheese burger　双层奶酪汉堡
KFC　肯德基炸鸡
Pizza　比萨

C. Wine List　酒水名

1) General　通用名
aperitif　餐前酒/开胃酒
beer　啤酒
bitter beer　苦啤酒
black beer　黑啤酒
brandy　白兰地
champagne　香槟酒
cocktail　鸡尾酒
dark beer　黑啤酒
draught beer　生啤酒
liqueur　餐后甜酒（利口酒）
rice wine　米酒，黄酒
rum　朗姆酒
sake　日本米酒，清酒
sherry　雪梨酒
vodka　伏特加
whisky　威士忌
white spirit　白酒
wine　葡萄酒

2) Beer　啤酒
Blue Ribbon　蓝带

Budweiser　百威
Carlsberg　嘉士伯
Heineken　喜力
Kirin　麒麟
San Miguel　生力
Tsingdao Beer　青岛
Suntory　三得利
Tiger　虎牌

3) Brandy　白兰地
Remy Martin V. S. O. P.　人头马
Hennessy　轩尼诗
Martell's X. O.　马爹利
Martell's 3 Star　马爹利三星

4) Chinese Alcoholic Drinks　中国酒
Bamboo Leaf　竹叶青
Fen Chiew　汾酒
Great Wall Wine　长城干红葡萄酒
Mou Tai/Maotai　茅台
Shaoxing Rice Wine　绍兴米酒
Xifeng Wine　西凤酒

D. Describing Food　食物的描述

冷（盘、菜）　cold
热（盘、菜）　hot
生的　raw
熟的　cooked
干的　dried
油腻的　fat

清淡的　light
味重的　heavy
新鲜的　fresh
辣的　spicy
腌渍的　pickled
咸的　salty

25

熏制的	smoked	煸	stir-fried
酸的	sour	爆	quick-fried
甜的	sweet	炸	deep-fried
苦的	bitter	煎	pan-fried
烹调术	cookery	焙；烤，烘	roasted
色、香、味	color, aroma and taste	清蒸	steamed
佐料	seasoning	汆	quick-boiled
刀功	slicing technique	熏	smoked
清炒	plain-fried	腌	salted

2. Interpreting Formulas

[1] 今天我请你吃饭。 I would like to invite you for dinner today.

[2] 附近好吃的地方不少，吃粤菜如何？ There are many nice places where we can eat. How about Cantonese food?

[3] 给你来杯红茶好吗？ Can I get you a cup of Chinese red tea?

[4] 不能让你买单，应该我请你，你是客人。 I can't let you pay. It is my treat, you are my guest.

[5] 我们休息一下，喝杯咖啡如何？ May I propose that we break for coffee now?

[6] 对不起，我出去一下。 Excuse me. I'll be right back.

[7] 请稍候，我去去就来。 Excuse me a moment.

[8] 您想喝什么酒？啤酒、红酒还是白酒？ What would you like to drink, beer, wine or liquor?

[9] 评判中餐烹调的优劣可依据中餐的三大要素，即"色、香、味"。 The three essential factors, or key elements, by which Chinese cooking is judged are known as "color, aroma and taste".

[10] 色、香、味这三要素的高品质，只有通过选料、调料、适时烹调、把握火候、装盘上桌这些微妙步骤的细心协调，才能取得。 These three essential elements, "color", "aroma", "taste", are achieved by the careful coordination of a series of delicate activities: selecting ingredients, mixing flavor, timing the cooking, controlling the heat and finally, laying out the food on the plate for the table.

[11] 在中国，共食一碗菜的习俗有助于家庭成员之间的团结和友谊。当然，在一些卫生意识比较强的地方，人们在共食放在餐桌中央的菜肴时，必须使用"公筷"或"公用"汤匙，以防疾病传染。 In China, the traditional ritual of sharing the food from the same dish plates is conducive to family

Chapter 4　Dining & Cuisine 宴请口译

togetherness and friendship. In more health-conscious environments, however, "public" chopsticks and spoons are used to remove food from the plates in the middle of the dining table, so as to prevent any possible spread of diseases.

[12] 中国人民与世界各族人民都有一个相同的基本观念, 即亲朋好友相聚, 美酒佳肴相敬, 实属人生之最大快乐也。　There is one key concept that the Chinese share with the rest of the world. That is, fine food and good drink, taken in the company of good friends, constitute one of the supreme pleasures in life.

[13] 在中国宴席上, 人们往往以"干杯"的方式互相敬酒。"干杯"的意思是一口喝干杯中的酒。"干"了"杯"中的酒, 表示敬人的心诚和相聚的欢乐。　In Chinese banquet, people will usually "Gan Bei" when toasting each other. "Gan Bei" means to raise up one's glass and drink it all the way down so that the glass is "dried up to the last drop". People dry up their glasses to communicate the message to guests that they are sincere in respecting guests and joyful in friendly gathering.

Ⅲ. Liaison Interpreting Practice

Dialogue 1
Scenario: *Ordering Food in a Western Food Restaurant*　西餐点菜

A: 晚上好！想吃点什么？
B: Have you got anything light to start the meal with?
A: 有的。这是我们的开胃小菜菜单。要不来点酸黄瓜？
B: Fine, we'll have some.
A: 主菜要什么？
B: Do you have any specials this evening?
A: 有的, 我们牛排加烤土豆不错！
B: OK. I'd like to have that.
A: 要什么甜点吗？我们的香草冰淇淋不错！
B: No, thanks!
A: 要喝点什么酒水？
B: Red wine, please.
A: 好的, 谢谢！

联络口译

Dialogue 2
Scenario: *Hosting a Dinner* 主人宴请

A: 杰克逊先生,请这边走。您请坐。

B: Thank you. It's really very kind of you to invite me to dinner.

A: 你能赏光,我很荣幸。你远道而来,参访我们公司,我们深感荣幸。愿我们的合作能有一个良好的开端!

B: You can be sure of that. Thank you for your friendliness and hospitality!

A: 我们今天吃中国菜,希望你会喜欢。

B: That's great! Chinese food is well-known to the world. I'm so lucky that I can taste them here in China.

A: 你想喝什么酒?啤酒、红酒还是白酒?

B: Beer, please.

A: 杰克逊先生,我提议为我们的友谊和合作干杯。

B: OK. To our friendship and cooperation. Cheers!

Dialogue 3
Scenario: *Enjoying Chinese Food* 品尝中国美食

A: I wonder how you Chinese appreciate Chinese food.

B: 评判中餐烹调的优劣,我们一般依据"色、香、味"。

A: That's interesting! How do you judge the color of food?

B: "色"作为"色、香、味"三要素中的首要标准,充分体现在宴会菜肴的装盘、摆放图案上。

A: And aroma?

B: "香"不仅是指鼻子对食物的直接感受,它还包括所选香料的新鲜程度以及佐料的合理调配。

A: Then taste?

B: "味"即恰到好处的调味艺术,当然它也包括食物的质地以及切菜的刀工。

A: That's amazing! How can the cook achieve the combination of the three?

B: 色、香、味这三要素的高品质,只有通过选料、调料、适时烹调、把握火候、装盘上桌这些微妙步骤的细心协调,才能取得。

A: Could you tell me about the custom of drinking in Chinese banquets?

Chapter 4　Dining & Cuisine 宴请口译

B：好的。在中国宴席上，人们往往以"干杯"的方式互相敬酒。"干杯"的意思是一口喝干杯中的酒。"干"了"杯"中的酒，表示敬人的心诚和相聚的欢乐。

A：Do we always have to "Gan Bei"? If so, I will get drunk soon.

B：也不尽然，外国宾客与中国东道主敬酒时，小啜一口也未尝不可。

Ⅳ. Notes for Interpreting

中餐菜名的口译方法：

　　在宴请饮食口译中，中餐菜名的口译是一个难点，主要是因为中国菜肴种类多样，且多具有丰富的文化意蕴。

　　中餐菜名口译的功能是：提供菜肴的主要原料、制作工艺或主要特色等客人选菜时所需要的基本信息。

　　中餐菜名口译的基本原则为：通常用名词词组来表达，以主要原料为中心词，制作工艺或方法用过去分词表示，主要特色用形容词表示，配料或佐料用带 with 或 in 的介词短语表示。

　　中餐菜名口译的主要方法包括直译法、意译法、音译法等。

　　意译法能比较充分地传达中餐菜名的文化意蕴，使用最为广泛。意译有四种具体方法：

　　1）以用料为主的翻译

　　A）主料 +（with）辅料，例如：

　　杏仁鸡丁　　chicken cubes with almond

　　牛肉豆腐　　beef with beancurd

　　西红柿炒蛋　　scrambled egg with tomato

　　B）主料 +（with/in）味汁，例如：

　　芥末鸭掌　　duck webs with mustard sauce

　　葱油鸡　　chicken in scallion oil

　　米酒鱼卷　　fish rolls with rice wine

　　2）以刀法为主的翻译

　　常用刀法的英语表达：切片 slicing，切丝 shredding，捣烂 mashing，切碎 mincing，切丁 dicing，切柳 filleting，酿入 stuffing 等。例如：

　　鱼片（sliced fish 或 fish slices）、肉丝（shredded meat 或 port shreds）、薯泥（mashed potatoes 或 potato mash）、肉碎或肉饼（minced meat 或 meat mince）、鸡丁（diced chicken 或 chicken cubes）、鱼柳（fillet of fish）、酿豆腐（stuffed bean curd）等。

3）以烹饪法为主的翻译

常用烹饪法的英语表达：煮（boiling）、煲、炖（stewing）、烧（braising）、蒸（steaming）、熏（smoking）、炸（frying）包括煎（pan-frying）、炒（stir-frying）、爆（quick-frying）、炸（deep-frying）、扒（frying and simmering）与回锅（twice-cooked stiring）等；

烘烤铁烧：铁烧（broiling; grilling）；烧烤（roasting）是在火上或在炉子里烧；烘（baking）是在密闭的烘具中烘，不与火直接接触，或在热的表面上烘；浇油烧（basting）是在烤肉上浇淋些油，防止烧焦。

白灼（scalding 或 blanching）：普遍用于烹制河鲜海味，如"白灼海螺片"（blanched sliced conch）、"白灼海虾"（scalded prawn）等。

译法示例：

A）烹法 + 主料（刀法）

软炸里脊　soft-fried pork fillet

烤乳猪　roast suckling pig

炒鳝片　stir-fried eel slices

B）烹法 + 主料（刀法）+（with）辅料

仔姜烧鸡柳　braised chicken fillet with tender ginger

C）烹法 + 主料（刀法）+（with, in）味汁

红烧牛肉　braised beef with brown sauce

鱼香肉丝　fried shredded pork with sweet and sour sauce

清炖猪蹄　stewed pig hoof in clean soup

4）以味道为主的翻译

A）刀法（口感）+ 主料 +（with）辅料

芝麻酥鸡　crisp chicken with sesame

陈皮兔丁　diced rabbit with orange peel

时蔬鸡片　sliced chicken with seasonal vegetables

B）口感 + 烹法 + 主料

香酥排骨　crisp fried spareribs

水煮嫩鱼　tender stewed fish

香煎鸡块　fragrant fried chicken

C）刀法（口感）+ 主料 +（with）味汁

茄汁鱼片　sliced fish with tomato sauce

椒麻鸡块　cutlets chicken with hot pepper

黄酒脆皮虾仁　crisp shrimps with rice wine sauce

音译法示例：
麻婆豆腐　Ma Po Tou Fu
东坡肉　Dong Po Pork
毛氏红烧肉　Chairman Mao's Stewed Pork with Soy Sauce
北京烤鸭　Beijing Roasted Duck
东江酿豆腐　Bean Curd Stuffed with Pork Mince，Dongjiang Style

Chapter 5　Exhibitions & Fairs　展会口译
口译主题：参展参会

I. Liaison Interpreting Tips

Brief Introduction to the World Expo 2010 Shanghai

World Expositions are galleries of human inspirations and thoughts. Since 1851 when the Great Exhibition of Industries of All Nations was held in London, the World Expositions have attained increasing prominence as grand events for economic, scientific, technological and cultural exchanges, serving as an important platform for displaying historical experience, exchanging innovative ideas, demonstrating esprit de corps and looking to the future.

With a long civilization, China favors international exchange and loves world peace. China owes its successful bid for the World Exposition in 2010 to the international community's support for and confidence in its reform and opening-up. The Exposition will be the first registered World Exposition in a developing country, which gives expression to the expectations the world's people place on China's future development.

So what will Expo 2010 Shanghai China deliver to the world? There is no doubt the Chinese people will present to the world a successful, splendid and unforgettable exposition.

Expo 2010 Shanghai China will be a great event to explore the full potential of urban life in the 21st century and a significant period in urban evolution. Fifty-five percent of the world population is expected to live in cities by the year 2010. The prospect of future urban life, a subject of global interest, concerns all nations, developed or less developed, and their people. Being the first World Exposition on the theme of city, Expo 2010 will attract governments and people from across the world, focusing on the theme "Better City, Better Life." For its 184 days, participants will display urban civilization to the full extent, exchange their experiences of urban development, disseminate advanced notions on cities and explore new approaches to human habitat, lifestyle and working conditions in the new century. They will learn how to create an eco-friendly society and maintain the sustainable development of human beings.

Expo 2010 Shanghai China will centre on innovation and interaction. Innovation is the soul, while cultural interaction is an important mission of the World Expositions. In the new era, Expo 2010 Shanghai China will contribute to human-centered development, scientific and technological innovation, cultural diversity and win-win cooperation for a better future, thus composing a melody with the key notes of highlighting innovation and interaction in the new century.

Expo 2010 Shanghai China will also be a grand international gathering. On the one hand, we shall endeavor to attract about 200 nations and international organizations to take part in the exhibition as well as 70 million visitors from home and abroad, ensuring the widest possible participation in the history of the World Expositions. On the other hand, we will put Expo 2010 Shanghai China in a global perspective and do our best to encourage the participation and gain the understanding and support of various countries and peoples, in order to turn Expo 2010 Shanghai China into a happy reunion of people from all over the world.

In addition, Expo 2010 Shanghai China will offer a wonderful opportunity for cross-culture dialogues. Before the conclusion of the Exposition, a "Shanghai Declaration" will be issued. This declaration, hopefully a milestone in the history of the World Expositions, will epitomize the insights to be offered by the participants and embody people's ideas for future cooperation and development and extensive common aspirations, thereby leaving a rich spiritual legacy of urban development to people throughout the world.

Ⅱ. Task-based Preparation

1. Useful Expressions

上海 2010 年世博会	the World Expo 2010 Shanghai (Expo 2010 Shanghai)
世博会会徽	the Expo emblem
"东方之冠"	The Crown of the East

联络口译

世博园区	the Expo Site
园区规划	site planning
用地范围	land use boundary
围栏区	enclosed area
园	park
区	area
片	zone
组	group
团	cluster
文化遗产	cultural heritage
文物保护	cultural relics preservation
建筑遗产	architectural heritage
平面图	master plan
结构图	structural plan
草图	sketch
中国馆	China's Pavilion
国家馆	National Pavilion
国际组织馆	International Organization Pavilion
主题馆	Theme Pavilion
企业馆	Corporate Pavilion
独立馆	Stand-alone Pavilion
联合馆	Joint Pavilion
自建馆	Self-built Pavilion
租赁馆	Rented Pavilion
广交会	Canton Fair
参观指南	exhibit directory
展品	exhibit
展位	booth
展览会	exhibition; fair
博览会	exposition
参展商	exhibitor
参展商手册	exhibitor manual
出口	export
出口许可证	export license
进口	import
进口许可证	import license
展览设施	facility
展馆平面图	floor plan
展馆地面接口	floor port
展厅	hall; pavilion
国际销售代理	international sales agent
特许经营	licensing
布展期	move-in
撤展期	move-out

2. Interpreting Formulas

[1] 世博会的主题是"城市,让生活更美好"。The theme of the Expo is "Better City, Better Life".

[2] 世博会将持续半年。The Expo will last six months.

[3] 世博会会徽看起来像三个人手挽着手。The Expo emblem looks like three people holding hands.

[4] 世博园区位于黄浦江两岸。The Expo Site is along both sides of the Huangpu River.

[5] 主题馆位于世博园区中心。The theme pavilions are in the center of the Expo Site.

[6] 你想坐磁悬浮列车还是专线大巴?Do you want to take the Maglev or the shuttle bus?

Chapter 5　Exhibitions & Fairs 展会口译

[7] 我们可以坐地铁或者轻轨。We can take the subway or the light rail.
[8] 展览正在成为上海一张重要的城市名片。Exhibition is becoming an important "city brand" of Shanghai.

Ⅲ. Liaison Interpreting Practice

Dialogue 1
Scenario：*Visiting the World Expo* 2010 *Shanghai*　参观世博会

1.1　Layout of the Expo Site　世博园区的规划布局

A：How is the Expo Site structured?
B：世博园区内的各类建筑会形成一道风景线，让人犹如身临未来的"地球村"。园区按照"园、区、片、组、团"五个层次进行结构布局。
A：That's impressive! What do you mean by "Park and Area"?
B："园"是指5.28平方公里的整个世博会园区规划用地范围。3.28平方公里的世博会围栏区被称为"区"，围栏区凭票进入。
A：How about "Zone, Group, Cluster"?
B：世博园区被划分为五个功能片区，称为"片"。五个功能片区分别用A、B、C、D、E编号标识方便记忆。"组"是指在每一个片区里的若干展馆组。每个展馆组可包含若干展馆"团"。

1.2　Major Spots in the Expo Site　世博会的主要参观点

A：Could you please tell me some of the major spots in the Expo Site?
B：好的。首先是世博会主题馆。上海世博会的主题涉及城市人、城市生命、城市星球，以及足迹、梦想五个概念领域，所以相对应设立了五个主题馆。其中"城市·人"馆、"城市·生命"馆和"城市·星球"馆三个主题馆位于浦东，使用新建展馆；"城市·足迹"馆和"城市·未来"馆位于浦西，使用原有工业建筑改造成的展馆。
A：Where is the China Pavilion?
B：中国馆位于浦东世博园区主入口的突出位置，世博会规划园区中围栏区的B片区，由中国国家馆、中国地区馆、港澳台馆三部分组成。
A：I heard a lot about it. What is special about it?
B：确实特别。中国馆建筑外观以"东方之冠"的构想主题表达中国文化的精神与气质。国家馆居中升起、层叠出挑，凝聚中国元素、象征中国精神；

地区馆水平展开，以舒展的平台基座的形态映衬国家馆成为开放、柔性、亲民、层次丰富的城市广场。

A：Is there any spot overseeing the whole site?

B：世博"和谐塔"位于未来馆的东面。登上和谐塔，你可以俯瞰上海世博会的园区全貌。

A：What other major spots will you recommend?

B：嗯，我会推荐：主题广场，在主题馆的西面；世博公园，位于世博园区浦东区域，与黄浦江相依；世博村，位于浦东世博园区的东北面；"城市最佳实践区"，设在浦西的 E 片区，靠近南浦大桥。

A：Sounds there are a lot to see. How can I find an easy way to visit all of them?

B：通过园区的高架平台，你可以方便地来回于各个展馆。

1.3　Pavilions of the Expo　世博会各类展馆

A：Apart from the National Pavilions, what other pavilions are there in the World Expo?

B：还有国际组织馆、主题馆、企业馆。

A：How many Corporate Pavilions are there?

B：企业馆历来是世博会上的一大展示亮点。这次上海世博会将有约 16 个企业馆。

A：It sounds amazing! How about the International Organization Pavilions, will they be attractive?

B：当然啦！国际组织馆的展示与国家馆同样精彩。

A：All pavilions are stand-alone buildings, aren't they?

B：不是的，参展者可以单独建馆，也可以联合建馆，还可以租赁由世博会组织者建造的展馆。

Dialogue 2

Scenario：*Visiting the Canton Fair*　广交会

A：It's my first time to visit the Canton Fair. Could you please make a general introduction about the Fair?

B：好的。广交会全称为"中国进出口商品交易会"，创办于 1957 年，每年春秋两季在广州举办，至 2010 年春季，已开展了 107 届。

Chapter 5　Exhibitions & Fairs 展会口译

A：Wow. That is a huge success! How can it be so successful?
B：广交会被誉为"中国第一展",是中国目前历史最久、层次最高、规模最大、商品种类最全、国别地区最广、到会客商最多、成交效果最好、信誉最佳的综合性国际贸易盛会。
A：That means it enjoys widest participation?
B：是的。每届广交会都有数千家资信良好、实力雄厚的外贸公司、生产企业、科研院所、外商投资企业、私营企业参展。
A：I can't wait to see it with my own eyes. Where is the site of the Fair?
B：在中国进出口商品交易会展馆,位于琶洲。

Dialogue 3
Scenario：*A Talk Between Sellers and Buyers in a Trade Fair*　展会客商交谈

A：早上好!欢迎来到广交会!
B：Thank you. What does your company deal with?
A：我们公司专营真丝地毯出口。
B：That's great! My company has a great interest in pure silk carpets.
A：您想要什么式样的?
B：Both the Chinese and the Turkish.
A：需要什么规格的呢?
B：Small wall carpets, say 4 feet by 3 feet. And would you tell me how many carpets you can manage to produce by early December?
A：这得看您想采购多少。
B：I would want 10,000.
A：量很大。恐怕我无法承诺到12月上旬能生产一万条,但是可以保证五千条。
B：Thank you. Now what is the price per piece?
A：这种地毯我们有固定批发价,每条30美元。
B：But we are dealing with a bulk purchase...
A：好吧,我们给你5%的折扣优惠。
B：That sounds nice.

Ⅳ. Notes for Interpreting

1. 中国馆的建筑外观以"东方之冠"的构想主题表达中国文化的精神与气质。国家馆居中升起、层叠出挑,凝聚中国元素、象征中国精神;地区馆水平展开,以舒展的平台基座形态映衬国家馆成为开放、柔性、亲民、层次丰富的城市广场。

　　本句口译的难点在于,句中有不少抽象表达,如"居中升起、层叠出挑"、"开放、柔性、亲民、层次丰富的"等。做好口译的第一步关键在于理解源语,即使源语是汉语,我们也要注意理解。对于源语中的抽象表达,要注意理解其实质意义,理解了实质意义,口译时就容易表达。"居中升起"指中国馆相对于地区馆的居中的位置,"层叠出挑"是中国传统建筑的斗拱形态,"开放、柔性、亲民、层次丰富的"意义不难理解,但要注意与建筑联系起来。全句译文如下:

　　The exterior design of the China Pavilion is based on the concept of "Oriental Crown", to express the spirit and disposition of Chinese culture. Rising from the center, the Chinese National Pavilion is supported by traditional *Dougong* brackets fixed layer upon layer, concentrating Chinese elements and embodying Chinese spirit. The Chinese Provinces Pavilion extends in flat under the Chinese National Pavilion, serving as a reliable platform, to build an open, mild, compatible and rich layered city square.

2. 广交会被誉为"中国第一展",是中国目前历史最久、层次最高、规模最大、商品种类最全、国别地区最广、到会客商最多、成交效果最好、信誉最佳的综合性国际贸易盛会。

　　在本句口译中,"中国第一展"容易错译为"China's First Fair",实际上,从其后多个"最"的表达可以看出,这里的"第一"不是时间上最早的意思,而是最好的意思。笔者曾见过某旅游景点"天下第一滩"译为"First Beach of the World",且不说汉语中的夸张表达是否应该直译,此处源语的意思亦理解错误,实际上"天下第一"意为"最好",应译为"Best Beach of the World"。

　　本句口译的一个难点在于多个排比结构的并列,口译时不容易把握好。排比铺陈是汉语表达中的一种常见现象,译员有必要学会处理好这类结构。一种办法是抓住一个核心信息,理出一个核心结构,其他表达皆服从于它。如本句可口译表达为:

　　The Canton Fair, with the longest history, **is the best** in level, scale, exhibit variety, buyer distribution, buyer attendance, business turnover and credit standing in China.

另一种译文为：The Canton Fair, comprehensive in nature, has won its fame of "China's No. 1 Fair" for the longest history, the highest level, the largest scale, the most complete exhibit variety, the broadest buyer distribution, the biggest buyer attendance, the greatest business turnover, and the best credit standing in China.

联络口译

Chapter 6　Business Negotiations　谈判口译
口译主题：商务洽谈

Ⅰ. Liaison Interpreting Tips

Niceties of Negotiation

What are the niceties in the nuances of negotiating? Here are some of the most commonly asked questions and answers.

What are some of the behaviors that undermine people when they negotiate?

The most common ploy is to overpower or intimidate the opposition through a variety of dirty tricks. But that leaves one side feeling used and abused, or even hostile, bitter, and angry. The other behavior that undermines the negotiating process is to focus on the relationship, to try to be nice and liked. While the likeability factor can play a role, giving you a better chance of achieving your goals if the opposing side likes you, you shouldn't let that get in the way of the negotiating process. Minding one's manners is not synonymous with playing doormat and having people walk all over you. You can be strong and still be courteous.

What are some of the ways to facilitate negotiations?

Respect time by being punctual and prepared. Work on your communication skills. Ask open-ended questions rather than issue pronouncements. Be careful of the word "why", though, because it can be perceived as accusatory. Invite discussion, and be open to correction and persuasion. "Please correct me if I'm wrong..." or "Help me to understand..." are much more likely to spur the negotiating process and give you valuable information than some pronouncement from your position platform. Analyze and improve upon ideas from the opposition's point of view. Ask their advice.

Chapter 6 Business Negotiations 谈判口译

When in doubt, use silence. It makes most people very uncomfortable. Just remember, he who speaks first loses.

Is negotiating in other cultures much different?

It most certainly is. Each culture has its own set of principles and values that determine how people think and behave. There is no generic international model, so there is a greater potential for misunderstanding because your opponent views the world differently. You heap issues on top of the issues on the table.

In which ways is negotiating in other cultures different?

First of all, there is the time issue. Not only must you allow a great deal more time for the entire process, but you must also deal with differing cultural time perspectives.

The opposing sides views on status, dignity, and protocol must also be factored in to the equation. Then there is the issue of language. You will need to explain a great deal more, and you will probably also have to work with an interpreter. You must be very careful of your choice of words, avoiding slang, jokes, and technical expressions... all of which can cramp your usual style. You must also be aware of cultural prejudices and stereotypes that the other side may hold. Remember, their values are different from yours.

And, on top of all that, you probably have to apply these differing behaviors to an entire negotiating team rather than an individual negotiator. Other cultures can be much more team-oriented than Americans with their strong sense of individuality.

What is the general principle for any negotiation?

Always leave on a positive note to maintain a working relationship for the future. Negotiations should maintain, if not improve, the relationship.

II. Task-based Preparation

1. Useful Expressions

发盘（发价）　　offer　　　　　　询盘（询价）　　inquiry
发实盘　　offer firm　　　　　　指示性价格　　price indication

中文	英文	中文	英文
速复	reply immediately	净价	net price
参考价	reference price	印花税	stamp duty
习惯做法	usual practice	含佣价	price including commission
交易磋商	business negotiation	货号	article No.
不受约束	without engagement	交货	delivery
业务洽谈	business discussion	装运（装船）	shipment
原样	original sample	装运港	port of shipment
复样	duplicate sample	卸货港	port of discharge
参考样品	reference sample	目的港	port of destination
代表性样品	representative sample	合同	contract
规格	specification	订约人	contractor
说明	description	订立合同	to enter into a contract
标准	standard type	签合同	to sign a contract
商品目录	catalogue	拟订合同	to draw up a contract
宣传小册	brochure; pamphlet	起草合同	to draft a contract
批发价	wholesale price	会签合同	to countersign a contract
零售价	retail price	合同正本	originals of the contract
运费	freight	合同副本	copies of the contract
金额	amount	书面合同	a written contract
关税	customs duty	做些让步	to make some concessions

2. Interpreting Formulas

[1] 我们的产品在国际市场上具有竞争力。 Our product is competitive in the international market.

[2] 顾客对我们的产品和服务评价甚高。 Our product and service has been very well-received by our customers.

[3] 如果对某些细节有意见的话，请提出来。 If you have any questions on the details, feel free to ask.

[4] 如果您有什么意见的话，我们还可以对计划稍加修改。 If you want to make any changes, minor alternations can be made then.

[5] 您能考虑接受我们的提案吗？ Could you consider accepting our counterproposal?

[6] 我们必须强调这些付款条件对我们很重要。 We must stress that these payment terms are very important to us.

[7] 请了解这一点对我们至关重要。 Please be aware that this is a crucial issue to us.

Chapter 6　Business Negotiations 谈判口译

[8]　我不知道您是否了解，但是这个条件对我们是必要的。　I don't know whether you realize it, but this condition is essential to us.

[9]　我们可以签合同了吗？　Are we anywhere near a contract?

[10]　我想我们都愿意签合同，因此双方都要做些让步。　I guess we both want to sign a contract, and we have to make some concessions to do it.

[11]　我们会准备好合同签字。　We'll have the contract ready for signature.

[12]　我们现有合同快要期满了，需要再谈一个新合同。　Our current contract is about to expire, and we'll need to discuss a new one.

Ⅲ. Liaison Interpreting Practice

Dialogue 1

Scenario： *Initial Business Talk*　初步洽谈

A：很高兴认识您，史密斯先生。我是销售代表，我姓王，这是我的名片。不知是否能帮到您？

B：Yes, I'm interested in your range of toys for children.

A：好的。这里有一些新的样品：右边的是机械玩具、电子玩具、电动玩具和智能玩具，适合5岁以上的孩子；左边的是竹木玩具、塑料玩具和毛绒玩具，适合5岁以下的孩子。这些都有现货。

B：Quite interesting.

A：这些玩具刚上市几个月，但是很受欢迎。

B：How about the prices?

A：这是价目表。

B：Thank you. What about delivery time?

A：我们收到订单后几天之内即可发货。

B：Can you give me a good discount on a large order?

A：嗯，这得看订购的量，具体我得查核一下。您可以稍候吗？请看看我们的产品宣传册。

B：Not at all. Thank you.

Dialogue 2

Scenario： *Bargaining in Negotiations*　讨价还价

A：既然大家都到齐了，我们正式开始吧。

B：OK. I'm sorry to say that the price you quote is too high. It would be very difficult for us to push any sales if we buy it at this price.

A：如果你考虑一下质量，你就不会觉得我们的价格太高了，况且，原材料的价格也上涨了。

B：Why not try meeting each other half way.

A：好的。这种产品你们想订多少？

B：I want to order 500 dozen.

A：如果你们订单下大些，我们价格也可以优惠点。

B：Then I'll increase my order to 900 dozen.

A：好的，我们给你9折优惠价。

B：Good. I can accept that. The next thing I'd like to bring up for discussion is packing. You know, packing has a close bearing on sales.

A：请陈述你的意见。

B：We wish the new packing will give our clients satisfaction. Buyers always pay great attention to packing. And we wish our opinions will be passed on to your manufacturers.

A：没问题。你方希望怎样发运货物，铁路还是海运？

B：By sea, please. Because of the high cost of railway transportation, we prefer sea transportation.

A：我们正是这么想的。

B：When can you effect shipment? I'm terribly worried about late shipment.

A：我们最晚在今年12月或明年初交货。

B：That's good.

Dialogue 3

Scenario：*Signing the Contract* 签订合同

A：早上好！我带来了草拟的合同，请您阅览。

B：OK. Sit down, please! What would you like, tea or coffee?

A：谢谢！请给我一杯茶。

B：Here you are.

（B看合同）

A：看完了吗？

B：Yes, I have one question about Clause 8. Are these the terms that we agreed on?

A：是的，我们来看看。

B：10 percent down and the balance at the time of shipment?

A：是的，我想那是我们所订的啊。

B：I'll need a few minutes to check over my notes again.

（B 查阅谈判记录）

A：对吗？

B：Yes. It is right.

A：您愿意现在签合同吗？

B：Sure. Where shall I put my signature?

A：最后一页上。我们签署两份正本，一份中文，一份英文，两份具有同等效力。

B：OK. Is that all?

A：行了。很高兴我们的谈判结果很圆满！

B：I hope this will lead to further business between us. All we have to do now is shake hands.

A：好的，我们出去喝一杯庆祝一下吧。

B：That's a great idea.

Ⅳ. Notes for Interpreting

1. 在双方谈判的过程中，一定要注意倾听对方的发言。

    如果对对方的观点表示了解，可以说：I see what you mean.（我明白您的意思。）如果表示赞成，可以说：

    That's a good idea.（是个好主意。）

    或者说：I agree with you.（我赞成。）

    如果是有条件的接受，可以用 on the condition that 这个句型，例如：

    We accept your proposal, on the condition that you order 20,000 units.（如果您订 2 万件，我们会接受您的建议。）

2. 在与外商，尤其是欧美国家的商人谈判时，如果有不同意见，最好坦率地提出来，而不要拐弯抹角。

    比如，表示无法赞同对方的意见时，可以说：I don't think that's a good idea.（我认为这点不妥。）

    或者说：Frankly, we can't agree with your proposal.（坦白地讲，我无法同意您的提案。）

    如果是拒绝，可以说：We're not prepared to accept your proposal at this time.（我们这一次不准备接受你们的建议。）

    有时，还要讲明拒绝的理由，如：To be quite honest, we don't believe this

product will sell very well in China.（说老实话，我们不相信这种产品在中国会卖得好。）

3. 谈判期间，由于言语沟通问题，出现误解也是在所难免的。有时可能是对方误解了你，有时可能是你误解了对方。

在这两种情况出现后，你可以说：

No, I'm afraid you misunderstood me. What I was trying to say was...（不，恐怕你误解了。我想说的是……）

或者说：Oh, I'm sorry, I misunderstood you. Then I go along with you. （哦，对不起，我误解你了。那样的话，我同意你的观点。）

Chapter 7　Business Etiquette　商务礼仪

口译主题：参观访问

Ⅰ. Liaison Interpreting Tips

International Business Etiquette

Etiquette is about presenting yourself with the kind of polish that shows you can be taken seriously. Etiquette is also about being comfortable around people (and making them comfortable around you!)

Most behavior that is perceived as disrespectful, discourteous or abrasive is unintentional, and could have been avoided by practicing good manners or etiquette. We've always found that most negative experiences with someone were unintentional and easily repaired by keeping an open mind and maintaining open, honest communication. Basic knowledge and practice of etiquette is a valuable advantage, because in a lot of situations, a second chance may not be possible or practical.

There are many written and unwritten rules and guidelines for etiquette, and it certainly behooves a business person to learn them. The caveat is that there is no possible way to know all of them!

These guidelines have some difficult-to-navigate nuances, depending on the company, the local culture, and the requirements of the situation. Possibilities to commit a faux pas are limitless, and chances are, sooner or later, you'll make a mistake. But you can minimize them, recover quickly, and avoid causing a bad impression by being generally considerate and attentive to the concerns of others, and by adhering to the basic rules of etiquette. When in doubt, stick to the basics.

The Basics

The most important thing to remember is to be courteous and thoughtful to the people around you, regardless of the situation. Consider other people's feelings, stick to your convictions as diplomatically as possible. Address conflict as situation-related, rather than person-related. Apologize when you step on toes. You can't go too far wrong if you stick with the basics you learned in Kindergarten. (Not that those basics are easy to remember when you're in a hard-nosed business meeting!)

This sounds simplistic, but the qualities we admire most when we see them in people in leadership positions, those are the very traits we work so hard to engender in our children. If you always behave so that you would not mind your spouse, kids, or grandparents watching you, you're probably doing fine. Avoid raising your voice (surprisingly, it can be much more effective at getting attention when lower it!) using harsh or derogatory language toward anyone (present or absent), or interrupting. You may not get as much "airtime" in meetings at first, but what you do say will be much more effective because it carries the weight of credibility and respectability.

Guidelines and Tips

It is important to note that etiquette in other cultures requires a bit of adaptation and flexibility. If you're travelling on business to a foreign destination, or have visitors here, it is a good idea to learn as much as you can about the culture they are coming from and make appropriate allowances.

Generally speaking, as long as you are trying to be considerate and express an interest in learning, you should be fine. If in doubt, err on the conservative, formal side.

1) *Meetings*

If a subject is important enough to call a meeting, be considerate of the participant's time and ensure that it is well-prepared.

Communicate beforehand: a. The objective; b. The expected duration (Be sure to observe the ending time scrupulously, unless everyone agrees to continue.); c. Items expected to be discussed.

Chapter 7 Business Etiquette 商务礼仪

Often overlooked—be sure to THANK meeting members for their time and participation, and demonstrate (in the minutes or written record, at least) how their contributions helped meet the objective of the meeting. Participants are frequently left wondering if they've been heard or if their attendances and contributions were noticed. Distribute minutes or some written record (no matter how simple the meeting) to all attendees and absentees, with concise but complete descriptions of decisions made and including action items.

Never assign an action item to a person who is not present to negotiate it, unless you absolutely have to. Note in the minutes that the person hasn't been notified, and will be contacted for a final disposition of the item.

2) *The Phone*

Always return calls. Even if you don't yet have an answer to the caller's question, call and explain what you're doing to get the requested information, or direct them to the appropriate place to get it.

If you're going to be out, have someone pick up your calls or at a minimum, have your answering system tell the caller when you'll be back in the office and when they can expect a call back.

When you initiate a call and get a receptionist or secretary, identify yourself and tell them the basic nature of your call. That way, you'll be sure you're getting the right person or department and the person you're trying to reach will be able to pull up the appropriate information and help you more efficiently.

When you're on the receiving end of a phone call, identify yourself and your department. Answer the phone with some enthusiasm or at least warmth, even if you ARE being interrupted, the person on the other end doesn't know that!

Make sure your voice mail system is working properly and doesn't tell the caller that the mailbox is full, transfer them to nowhere, or ring indefinitely. Address technical and system problems—a rude machine or system is as unacceptable as a rude person.

You don't have to reply to obvious solicitations. If someone is calling to sell you something, you can indicate that you are not interested and hang up without losing too much time on it. However, you do need to be careful. You may be receiving a call from an insurance or long distance company that wants to hire you as a consultant! Be sure you know the nature of the call before you (politely, of course) excuse yourself.

Personalize the conversation. Many people act in electronic media (including phone, phone mail, and e-mail) the way they act in their cars. They feel since they're not face-to-face with a person, it is perfectly acceptable to be abrupt, crass, or rude. We need to ensure that we make best use of the advantages of these media without falling headfirst into the disadvantages.

3) E-mails

Make the subject line specific. Think of the many messages you're received with the generic subject line, "Hi" or "Just for you."

Don't forward messages with three pages of mail—to information before they get to the content. In the message you forward, delete the extraneous information such as all the "Memo to," subject, addresses, and date lines.

When replying to a question, copy only the question into your e-mail, then provide your response. You needn't hit reply automatically, but don't send a bare message that only reads, "Yes." It's too blunt and confuses the reader.

Address and sign your e-mails. Although this is included in the To and From sections, remember that you're communicating with a person, not a computer.

Don't type in all caps. Too intense, and you appear too lazy to type properly. This is still a written medium. Follow standard writing guidelines as a professional courtesy.

4) Interruptions

Avoid interruptions (of singular or group work sessions, meetings, phone calls, or even discussions) if at all possible. Most management folks feel free to interrupt informal working sessions of subordinates, but need to realize that they may be interrupting a brainstorming session that will produce the company's next big success.

Always apologize if you must interrupt a conversation, meeting, or someone's concentration on a task. Quickly state the nature of what you need, and show consideration for the fact that you are interrupting valuable work or progress.

5) *Dress/Appearance*

It can be insulting to your coworkers or clients to show a lack of concern about your appearance.

Being wrinkled, unshaven, smelly or unkempt communicates (intentionally or not) that you don't care enough about the situation, the people or the company to present yourself respectably.

If in doubt, always err on the side of conservative. If you think jeans may be OK for a social event but aren't sure, show up in ironed khakis and a nice golf shirt. If you think a situation may call for dress slacks, wear a dress shirt and tie. If you have any inkling that a suit may be called for, dress to the nines.

Women's clothing is a bit more complicated, but again, err on the side of conservative and dressy.

This is a lot to consider, and there's a lot more out there in business etiquette. Volumes of information have been written on what is right and correct in business etiquette. It's enough to make veterans and newcomers too insecure to deal with people.

The important thing to remember is that if you strive to make the people around you feel comfortable and valued, you have succeeded whether you're perfectly in compliance with these or any rules you've read.

Ⅱ. Task-based Preparation

1. Useful Expressions

| 行程表 | schedule; itinerary | 市中心 | downtown area |
| 开发区 | development area/zone | 工业化 | industrialization |

城市化　urbanization
经济技术开发区　economic & technological development zone
高新技术产业开发区　hi-and-new-tech industrial development zone
出口加工区　export processing zone
保税区　free trade zone; bonded area

生态友好型的　eco-friendly
行政部门　administrative department
研发部　R&D department
生产线　production line
全自动的　fully-automated
质检　quality inspection; quality control

2. Interpreting Formulas

[1] Here's a copy of the itinerary of our tour today.　这是一份我们今天的行程安排表。

[2] According to our plan, today we will visit...　按照我们的行程安排，今天我们将参观……

[3] We'll set off at 8:30 in the morning.　我们早上8:30出发。

[4] How do you like this itinerary?　您觉得这个日程安排怎么样？

[5] OK, we can arrange that. How about...?　好的，我们可以安排。……（时间）怎么样？

[6] Sorry. We have to make some changes in our itinerary.　对不起，我们得对行程做个调整。

[7] We have to cancel the visit to...　我们不得不取消去……的参观。

[8] We feel very sorry about this.　对此我们非常抱歉。

[9] Our alternative plan is...　我们的新计划是……

[10] Thank you for your understanding.　谢谢您的理解。

[11] 广州开发区包括广州经济技术开发区、广州高新技术产业开发区、广州出口加工区和广州保税区。　Guangzhou Development District comprises four adjacent zones and they are: Guangzhou Economic & Technological Development District, Guangzhou Hi-Tech Industrial Development Zone, Guangzhou Export Processing Zone and Guangzhou Free Trade Zone.

[12] 看来是个宜商宜居的好地方啊。　It seems to be an ideal place both for business and residence.

[13] 我拿我们的小册子给您看看，好吗？　May I show you our brochure?

[14] 我给您看看介绍本公司和新产品的录像。　I'll show you a video introducing our company and new products.

[15] 请随意提问。　Please feel free to ask any questions.

Chapter 7   Business Etiquette 商务礼仪

[16] 我们的技术部门也许熟悉这个问题。   Our technical development may be familiar with the problem.

[17] 很抱歉，那是机密。我无法回答您的问题。   I'm sorry but that's confidential. I can't answer your question.

[18] 那很危险，请勿靠近。   That's dangerous. Please keep off.

[19] 参观过我们的工厂后，您的整体印象如何？   Having seen our plant, what's your overall impression?

[20] 我有信心我们能建立长期的商业关系。   I have confidence in establishing a long-term business relationship with you.

Ⅲ. Liaison Interpreting Practice

Dialogue 1
Scenario：*Discussing Schedule and Timetable*   商议日程计划时间表

1.1   Planning the Visit 计划行程

A：What places are we going to visit tomorrow?
B：给您我们的参观行程表。按计划，明天上午我们参观开发区。
A：What about afternoon?
B：下午我们参观市中心。
A：OK. When shall we start our journey tomorrow morning?
B：我8点到宾馆接您。我们8点半出发，可以吗？
A：OK. How long will the whole trip take?
B：我看一下，大约9个或10个小时。我们争取下午6点回来。

1.2   Asking for Opinions about the Itinerary 询问对日程安排的意见

A：您觉得这个日程安排怎么样？
B：It's very good on the whole, but can we possibly make some small changes?
A：当然可以，想做什么调整？
B：Could you please arrange a visit to your factory?
A：好的，我们可以安排。后天去如何？
B：All right. Thank you.
A：不用客气。

联络口译

Dialogue 2

Scenario: *Director Li Is Introducing the Guangzhou Development District to Foreign Visitors.* 开发区李主任向外宾介绍"广州开发区"。

A: In which part of the city does the Guangzhou Development District lie?

B: 广州开发区位于广州市东部,是广州近年发展的重中之重。

A: Why does it become so important?

B: 广州构建其都会区的基本发展战略为:"南拓、北优、东进、西联"。广州作为东部的中心,是推进广州工业化、城市化的主要力量。

A: How big is the district?

B: 广州开发区包括广州经济技术开发区、广州高新技术产业开发区、广州出口加工区和广州保税区。这四个区都是经国务院批准设立的首批国家级经济功能区,自2002年联合办公运作。

A: Four in one. I guess that is special!

B: 是的,四合一的管理模式意味着我们开发区有着独特的竞争优势。

A: Could you elaborate on that?

B: 当然可以。我们的主要竞争优势在于:管理体制精干高效;投资领域广,容纳项目类型广;地缘区位优势明显;基础设施完善等。

A: It seems to be an ideal place both for business and residence.

B: 确实是。我们的目标是把开发区建成综合制造业基地、高新技术开发和生产基地、交通和物流设施完备的服务业基地和生态友好型的宜居之地。

Dialogue 3

Scenario: *Visiting the Factory* 参观工厂

A: 我陪您到各处看看,边走边讲解生产操作。

B: That'll be most helpful.

A: 那是我们的办公大楼。我们所有的行政部门都在那里。那边是研发部。

B: How much do you spend on development every year?

A: 大约是总销售额的3%到4%。

B: What's that building opposite us?

A: 那是仓库,存放周转快的货物,这样当有急的订货时,就可以立刻交现货。

B: If I placed an order now, how long would it be before I got delivery?

Chapter 7　Business Etiquette 商务礼仪

A：那主要得依据订单大小以及你需要的产品而定。好的,我们到生产车间了。请戴上安全帽。
B：OK.
A：请留神脚下。
B：Thank you. Is the production line fully-automated?
A：嗯,不是全自动的。
B：I see. How do you control the quality?
A：所有产品在整个生产过程中都必须通过五道质检关。
B：What's the monthly output?
A：目前每月产量1 000套,但从明年开始每月1 200套。
B：What's your usual percentage of rejects?
A：正常情况下为0.2%左右。
B：That's wonderful. Is that where the finished products come off?
A：是的。现在我们稍微休息一下吧。
B：It was very kind of you to give me a tour of the place. It gave me a good idea of your product range.
A：带我们的客户来参观工厂是我们的荣幸。不知道你总体印象如何?
B：Very impressive, indeed, especially your quality controls. Could you give me some brochures of your products? And the price list if possible.
A：好的。这是我们的销售目录和说明书。
B：Thank you.

Ⅳ. Notes for Interpreting

1. 广州构建其都会区的基本发展战略为:"南拓、北优、东进、西联"。

　　汉语中常用缩略语表达,如本句中的"南拓、北优、东进、西联"。汉语的缩略语表达在口译时一定要注意理解其代表的完整意思,当然,要做到确切的理解与译员的汉语古文功底不无关系,如本句中的"拓、优、进、联"分别代表拓展、优化、推进和联动协调。本句可译为:
　　The fundamental strategy of Guangzhou developing the metropolis areas is "exploration in the south, optimization in the north, extension in the east and co-ordination in the west".

2. 我们的主要竞争优势在于：管理体制精干高效；投资领域广，容纳项目类型广；地缘区位优势明显；基础设施完善等。

本句口译的难点在于排比结构，如上一章讲解的那样，在口译表达时，注意理清是以名词结构为中心还是以形容词结构为中心。本句可译为：

Our major competitive advantages are: a simple and efficient administrative structure, availability to all different investment modes and projects, advantageous geographic location and well-developed infrastructure.

口译初学者如果处理不了这么复杂的机构，采用如下这样删繁就简的办法也不失为一种对策：

We enjoy competitive advantages in administrative structure, investment range and modes, geographic location and infrastructure.

Chapter 8　Shopping in China　购物口译
口译主题：在中国购物

Ⅰ. Liaison Interpreting Tips

China boasts cheap but nice commodities and is regarded by foreign visitors as a "shopping paradise"（购物天堂）. Foreign visitors do shopping in China for two purposes: to buy necessities（生活必需品）for their tour and to purchase specialties in China（中国特产）for collection and as gifts for their family and friends.

When foreign guests need to buy necessities for their tour, it is advisable for you, the escort interpreter, to take them to supermarkets（大型超市）which are convenient and thus getting more and more popular in China.

If foreign guests want to purchase specialties in China for collection and as gifts for their family and friends, silk（丝绸）, pearls and jewels（珠宝）, antique and curio（古董）and handicrafts（手工艺品）are always of great interest to them. As the escort interpreter, you need to introduce about varieties, prices and features in order to help them make wise choices. It will be better if you tell them more cultural information about the specialty, which will surely add to the fun of their shopping experience in China.

You may also remind the foreign guests shopping in China to keep the receipt（收据）of the things they've bought, which they will need for customs inspection（海关检查）.

Ⅱ. Task-based Preparation

1. Useful Expressions

古玩　antique; curio　　　　　　镯子　bracelet
钱币　coin　　　　　　　　　　手链　chain bracelet

钻石	diamond	景泰蓝	cloisonné
耳环	earring	金饰	gold jewelry
项链	necklace	银饰	silver jewelry
戒指	ring	珍珠	pearl
坠子	pendant	珠宝；首饰	jewelry；jewels
装饰品	ornaments	工艺品商店	arts-and-crafts shop
铜器	copperware	原作	originals
陶器	pottery	复制品	reproductions
瓷器	chinaware；porcelain	松鹤图	picture of cranes with pine trees

2. Interpreting Formulas

[1] 我建议你买些有中国特色的东西。 I suggest you buy something typically Chinese.

[2] 景德镇以瓷器著称，又叫瓷都。 Jingdezhen is famous for chinaware, and it's called the capital of chinaware.

[3] 我相信它肯定会让你经常想起这次旅行的。 I'm sure it'll constantly remind you of your visit to this city.

[4] 你可以买点中国的手工艺品，如景泰蓝、陶器、瓷器或玉器等。 You can choose some Chinese arts and crafts, such as cloisonné, pottery, porcelain or jadeware.

[5] 如果你想买的话，可以到工艺品商店去。 You may go to an arts-and-crafts shop if you want to buy some.

[6] 我想你肯定是想找些有中国特色但又不太贵的东西，对吧？ I guess you want to find something typical Chinese, but not very dear. Am I right?

[7] 作为礼品，我觉得这个会很特别。 I think this would be quite unique as a present.

[8] 真的……，而假的…… The real is..., while the false is....

[9] 有什么特别中意的吗？ Is there anything that caters to your special taste?

[10] 你想要什么特别的东西？ Are you looking for anything special?

[11] 你要原作还是复制品？ Would you like to buy originals or reproductions?

[12] 我可以问一问，但一般来说，一分钱一分货。 I can ask them, but generally speaking, a higher price means better quality.

[13] 他们可以给你95折，你觉得可以接受吗？ They can give you 5% off. Do you think it's reasonable?

[14] 如果你在这家店消费超过300元，就可以享受10%的折扣。 You can enjoy 10% off if you spend more than 300 yuan in the store.

Chapter 8　Shopping in China 购物口译

Ⅲ．Liaison Interpreting Practice

Dialogue 1

Scenario：Introducing Specialties and Souvenirs　介绍购买特产和纪念品

A：I'd like to buy some good Chinese souvenirs for my friends.
B：你可以买些中国的工艺品，如景泰蓝、陶器、瓷器或玉器等。
A：I need to buy some gifts also for my daughter. What would you suggest?
B：我建议你买些有中国特色的东西。
A：Good idea. What do you suggest?
B：这只玉手镯怎么样？
A：Very beautiful. I'll take it. What are the specialties here?
B：嗯，是瓷器。这里有一个市叫景德镇，以瓷器著称，又叫"瓷都"。
A：That's great. One of my friends is fond of collecting chinaware. I can buy some for him.
B：好的，我们来选几件。
A：I really like the umbrellas the girls here carry around.
B：那干吗不买一把？我想它肯定会让你经常想起这次旅行的。
A：Which one do you think is the best?
B：我觉得这把紫色的带中国刺绣的不错。

Dialogue 2

Scenario：Shopping at a Jewelry, Arts-and-Crafts Shop　在珠宝店、工艺品店购物

A：Where can I get some traditional Chinese arts-and-crafts for my friends?
B：如果你想买的话，可以到工艺品商店去。宾馆附近就有一家。
A：How about going there now?
B：好的。我想你肯定是想找些有中国特色但又不太贵的东西，对吧？
A：You're right. What do you suggest?
B：嗯，景泰蓝项链如何？
A：I'm wondering whether my wife will like it.
B：我肯定她喜欢。作为礼品，我觉得景泰蓝项链很特别。
A：Don't you think this necklace is a bit old-fashioned?
B：不，这是最新的款式呢，您不觉得这个很优雅吗？

59

联络口译

A: Eh, I guess I will find something better than this. What else do you suggest I should buy?

B: 买几把檀香扇怎样？檀香扇气味芳香提神。

A: Oh, yes. I have heard of this kind of fan. Can you help me to tell real sandalwood?

B: 好的。真的檀香扇芳香自然，而假的檀香扇气味较浓，因为那种香是添加的。

A: Are all the fans of the same shape?

B: 不。你看，有不同的样式和大小。有方形的、圆形的，还有叶形的。

A: How much is the leaf-shaped sandalwood fan?

B: 人民币 100 元。

A: Is it the same price as those others?

B: 不是的。根据型号大小和式样不同，价格也有所差别。

Dialogue 3

Scenario: *Shopping at an Antique Shop*　在古董店选购

A: 您看，我们店里的古董多种多样。

B: Yes, and everything is so beautiful.

A: 有什么您特别中意的吗？

B: Well, I'm interested in Chinese paintings. Have you got any good ones?

A: 有，我们这有不少。你有什么特别的选择？

B: Yes. I'd like to buy some Chinese paintings with local flavor.

A: 这幅松鹤图怎么样？

B: Oh, I like it very much.

A: 您要原作还是复制品？

B: Please show me some originals first.

A: 好的，给您这幅。请慢慢看。

Dialogue 4

Scenario: *Bargaining While Buying Silk*　买丝绸讲价

A: I've heard that Chinese silk is famous for its original design and fine quality. Where can I buy some?

B: 在任何大型商场的丝绸部都能买到。

Chapter 8　Shopping in China 购物口译

A：Shall we go and have a look?
B：好的，我很乐意。
A：I have never seen anything so special.
B：是的，丝绸不仅好看，而且手感也好。
A：What can silk be used for?
B：可以用来做旗袍、手帕、衬衫等。
A：Cheongsam?! That's very typical of Chinese! What kind of silk is suitable for making a cheongsam?
B：最好是买那种稍厚耐磨的。
A：Is this kind of silk washable?
B：可以。这种丝绸是经过特殊技术特别处理的，不会缩水。
A：I like it, but it's a little bit expensive. Do they have any at a lower price?
B：我可以问一问，但是一般来说，一分钱一分货。
A：That's right, but I still think it's a bit expensive. I wonder if they can give me a discount.
B：他们说，如果您在这家店消费超过300元，就可以享受10%的优惠折扣。

联络口译

Chapter 9　Seeing Guests Off　送客礼仪
口译主题：送客道别

I. Liaison Interpreting Tips

　　Your foreign guests are leaving China or for other cities, which means you will be relieved from your work soon. Your last job is seeing-off（送行）.

　　It is always appreciated to help your foreign guests pack up their luggage and confirm their flight time and number.

　　The exit procedures include frontier inspection（边防检查）, customs inspection（海关检查）and security checks（安全检查）. At the airport, your foreign guests need to get the boarding pass（登机牌）, do customs declaration（海关申报）and go through luggage check（行李检查）and security check（安检）before boarding the flight.

　　If your foreign guests have nothing to declare, they can go through the green channel（绿色通道）. For those who need to do customs declaration, they will have to fill in the declaration form（海关申报单）and go through the red channel（红色通道）. You may help them identify which items in their luggage is dutiable（需要交税）, how much the tariff rate（税率）is and where to pay the duty（缴纳关税）.

II. Task-based Preparation

1. Useful Expressions

送行　seeing-off
饯行　farewell dinner
表达良好祝愿　to express good will
纪念品　souvenir
特产　specialties
中国茶　Chinese tea

剪纸　paper-cutting
临行当天　departure date
办理出境手续　to go through the customs procedures/formalities
海关人员　customs officers
海关检查　customs inspection

Chapter 9　Seeing Guests Off 送客礼仪

边防检查　frontier inspection
移民局工作人员　immigration officers
出境登记卡　departure permit
交验护照　passport checks
检查签证　visa checks
申报单　declaration form
要交税的　dutiable
免税的　duty-free
安全检查　security checks

关税申报单　customs declaration
外币申报单　currency declaration
出境卡　departure card
贵重物品　valuables
易腐烂物品　perishables
绿色通道　green channel
烟酒　cigarettes and liquor
超过限额　exceed the quota

2. Interpreting Formulas

［1］ I'm planning a farewell dinner for you.　我正准备为您饯行呢。

［2］ Let's drink to our friendship! Cheers!　为我们的友谊喝一杯吧，干杯！

［3］ I'm very glad that you enjoyed your stay here.　我很高兴你能在这儿过得很愉快。

［4］ Please accept this little present as a souvenir from China.　请收下这份小礼物作为中国之行的纪念吧。

［5］ Have you finished your packing yet?　你的行李都准备好了吗？

［6］ Would you please check your passport, ticket and luggage?　请再检查一下您的护照、机票和行李，好吗？

［7］ Let me handle your luggage.　我来帮你拿行李吧。

［8］ You should first fill out the declaration form.　你得先填写出境旅客申报单。

［9］ If you have nothing to declare, you can go through the green channel.　如果你没有什么要申报的，可以直接走绿色通道。

［10］ You need to show them your passport, China departure card and some customs forms.　你得出示一下您的护照、中国出境卡和海关的一些表格。

［11］ You can ask the customs officers for the forms.　你可以向海关工作人员索要那些表格。

［12］ Tourists are allowed to take out a limited amount of gifts.　游客可以带一定数量的礼品出境。

［13］ The export of paintings before the Qing Dynasty is prohibited.　清代以前的古画是禁止出口的。

［14］ Perishables like fruits are not allowed.　水果之类易腐烂的东西是不允许带的。

［15］ I'm afraid you'll have to pay taxes on these things. They exceed the quota.　这些东西你得交税，它们超额了。

［16］ You're allowed 800 yuan duty free.　允许带 800 元的免税品。

[17] It's my pleasure to have been your guide and interpreter. I'm glad I could help. 我很荣幸担任了您的导游和翻译，很高兴我能帮得上您。

[18] Have a pleasant journey! Happy landing! 祝你旅途愉快！一路平安！

Ⅲ. Liaison Interpreting Practice

Dialogue 1

Scenario: *Seeing off a Foreign Guest* 送行

A: How time flies! I'll go back to the States soon. I really enjoyed the tour in China.
B: 我正准备为您饯行呢。
A: That's very kind of you. Thank you for helping me so much during my stay in China.
B: 我很乐意。为我们的友谊喝一杯吧。干杯！
A: Cheers! Chinese food is so delicious. I will miss it.
B: 那您多吃点。我很高兴您能在这儿过得很愉快。请收下这份小礼物作为中国之行的纪念吧。
A: Wow, It's really beautiful! Thank you very much.
B: 希望这份礼物能让你想起愉快的中国之行。
A: Surely I will.
(At the front gate of the hotel.)
B: 您的行李都准备好了吗？
A: Yes, I'm ready to go now.
B: 好的。请再检查一下您的护照、机票和行李，好吗？
A: All right. Here comes a taxi. Let's go.
B: 好的。我来帮您拿行李吧。

Dialogue 2

Scenario: *Introducing Customs Formalities* 介绍海关手续

A: Is there anything special about the procedures at the Customs here?
B: 没什么特别的。您只需出示您的护照、中国出境卡和海关的一些表格。
A: What kind of forms do I need here?
B: 一般来说，需要填关税申报单和外币申报单。您可以向海关工作人员索要这些表格。
A: What's the procedure for customs declaration?

Chapter 9　Seeing Guests Off 送客礼仪

B：您得先填写出境旅客申报单，外币、金银等贵重物品必须填写。
A：Where should I go through the Customs if I have nothing to declare?
B：如果您没有什么要申报的，可以直接走绿色通道。
A：I have bought some gifts for my friends. Are they dutiable?
B：那得看情况。旅客可以带一定数量的礼品出境。
A：I bought some silk products for my friends. Should I pay duty for them?
B：多少钱的？
A：About 500 yuan.
B：允许带 800 元的免税品，因此不用交税。
A：How about the emerald necklace?
B：那个不能免税，恐怕您得交税了。
A：How about the old Chinese painting I've bought. Is it dutiable?
B：哦，那是清朝的，不用交税即可携带出境。
A：Are all Chinese paintings duty free?
B：也不一定。清代以前的古画是禁止出口的。
A：I have some cigarettes for my own use.
B：这些东西超过配额了，您得交税。

Dialogue 3

Scenario：*Saying Goodbye and Bidding Farewell*　道别

A：I guess it's time to say goodbye now. I'd like to thank you again for all you've done for me.
B：我很荣幸担任了您的导游和翻译，很高兴我能帮得上您。
A：Hope we can meet again some day.
B：我也一样。请保持联系。
A：Everything I've seen here has made a deep impression on me, including you.
B：谢谢！欢迎再来！
A：I hope you'll come to America some day.
B：我会的。谢谢！祝您旅途愉快！一路平安！

联络口译

Chapter 10　Cooperation Talks　国际合作
口译主题：教育合作

I. Liaison Interpreting Tips

Beginning from this chapter, readers will find that the interpreting practice is gaining its difficulty in terms of sentence/segment length and density of information. This being said, the following six chapters still fall into the domain of liaison interpreting in nature. The design of the chapters is to prepare interpreting students to get comfortable with longer and more difficult sentences, which are not uncommon in the real liaison interpreting task.

With the ever intensifying effects of globalisation, international cooperation in education is increasingly called upon by many open and liberalised counties. Liaison interpreting in this regard pertains to such scenarios as negotiation of domestic and foreign collaborative education programs, project coordination, seminars for overseas students and more. The register of utterance, therefore, falls into a continuum from colloquial to formal. Interpreters should be able to adjust their choices of words (or diction) in the target language to the degree of formality of the interpreting context. One immediate example is the interpretation of "your school". If this phrase takes place in a formal negotiation between the two sides, "贵校" sounds pleasant and polite to the hearers. If the phrase is an utterance in a students-based exchange program, "你所在的学府" will be polite and respectful enough. If the phase is for daily and less formal communication, "你的学校" will suffice.

As education cooperation is invariably related to cultural exchange, interpreters must prepare some culture-specific proper names for the interpreting event. For example, whenever Chinese culture is involved, the Confucius culture, traditional Chinese medicines (TCM), Chinese martial arts (or better known as Kong-fu), food and tea

Chapter 10 Cooperation Talks 国际合作

cultures are constantly referred to and discussed. And courses centring on these subject matters are usually popular outside China, thus a frequent topic for Sino-foreign cooperation in education. It is advisable that interpreters learn the proper names and expressions by heart.

Another problem is that speakers sometimes make obvious mistakes. To an educated audience, should interpreters interpret the erroneous statements or correct them? Generally speaking, interpreters are required to be faithful to the speakers and interpret the statements as they are, however mistaken they seem. This said, interpreters should be flexible to cope with different situations. For a slip of tongue, which is not intended by the speaker, interpreter may ask for clarification before starting interpreting. If speakers insist on the erroneous statements, interpreters then are supposed to interpret without correcting them.

Last but not least, interpreters ought to remember the names of universities and institutions and the names of the colleges thereof, because in the West, a college or a school in a university is usually named after a famous person (e.g. College of Central Saint Martin, Merton College, and Lincoln College). This is not same in China, where colleges and schools are normally named by the subjects (e.g. School of Interpreting and Translation Studies, College of Life Science, College of Journalism and Communication).

II. Task-based Preparation

1. Useful Expressions

高见 insights
cripple 挫败
师资 teaching quality/faculty members

留学生 oversea students
constantly evolving 一直在改进完善
vibrant 活泼生动
性价比 price-to-performance ratio/tuition-to-quality ratio/tuition-and-quality balance

worth the price 物有所值
英镑兑人民币 pound against RMB
appreciation of RMB 人民币升值
compromise quality 牺牲质量/在质量上打折扣

孔子学院 Confucius Institute
多元文化 multi-cultures/diversified cultures

命题和考务　test question design and test administration
发挥……带动作用　play a leading role in promoting...
太极拳　Taichi/Shadow Boxing
少林拳　Shaolin Boxing
京剧　Peking Opera
公务员　civil servants
北京外国语大学　Beijing Foreign Studies University
罗马大学　University of Rome La Sapienza

2. Interpreting Formulas

[1] I would like to express my gratitude to... for joining us in the discussion of the cooperation between our universities.　我谨此感谢……参与商讨这次双方合作办学的事宜。

[2] The Diploma program provides the student with a possibility to continue their study at a Master level.　这一文凭项目可以提供学生升读硕士的机会。

[3] The teaching quality concerns many parents, so can you briefly tell us about the teaching team in your college?　许多学生家长很关心师资情况，能否简要介绍一下贵校的师资情况？

[4] With the teaching quality is assured, we are confident to deliver the "1+2" mechanism.　贵校师资实力有保证，我们就放心推行"1+2"的方案。

[5] The language skills you will gain should set you on the path for future success, wherever and whatever that may be.　无论你将来的目标是什么，你所习得的语言技能将助你走上成功之路。

[6] Can you give us a landscape of what British schools look like?　你能描述一些英国学校的概况吗？

[7] Will the booming quantity affect the quality of teaching?　会不会因学生数量增多而无暇顾及教学质量？

[8] ... is a non-profit language institution whose mission is to enhance...　……是一非营利语言推广机构，其宗旨在于促进……

[9] In the recruitment of Chinese directors and instructors, a strict screening process has been taken to ensure high quality.　在中方院长和教师的选派工作中，坚持严格把关、保证质量。

[10] Confucius Institutes have open up to communities by providing non-degree Chinese classes.　孔子学院面向社区开展非学历的汉语教学。

[11] Could you cite some examples to show that Chinese involvement in the Confucius Institute is a cooperation program of mutual benefits?　中方参与到孔子学院是一项互惠互利的合作项目，你能否举些例子来说明这一点？

Chapter 10 Cooperation Talks 国际合作

[12] The Confucius Institute should entail three centers, namely promotion centers, teaching and training centers, and exam and research centers. 今后孔子学院应建成"三个中心",即推广中心、教学和培训中心、考试和研究中心。

Ⅲ. Liaison Interpreting Practice

Dialogue 1

Scenario: The President (C) of a Chinese University Is Talking about the Cooperation Mechanism with His British Counterpart (E). Please Act as a Liaison Interpreter for the Discussion.

C: 我谨此感谢巴顿校长一行前来我校参与商讨这次双方合作办学的事宜。[1]

E: Well, certainly, the pleasure is mine. Your university has been very popular and prestige among Chinese students. It will be our immense honour to enrol some of your excellent students in my university.

C: 那我们就直接进入主题了。从我收到的备忘录上看,贵校将为我校学生开设三年制的课程。恐怕三年的专科对于中国学生竞争力不够,贵校在本科或是研究生教育上有其他方案吗?

E: The Diploma program provides the student with a possibility to continue their study at a Master level. By joining the Diploma program, students at their third year can **either** choose to sign up with a local university and follow up their higher study, **or** go abroad and have their Master at several universities in cooperation with our college. [2]

C: 好的,贵校在这方面确实很有优势,一方面为外国的大学与学院承认这一证书,另一方面也为学生提供国内专升本的途径,以使学生在国内更好地发展。

E: That's exactly what we are doing and we think this opens more doors for students.

C: 那么我们谈一下到底是"1+2"还是"2+2"的合作模式会好一些。贵方有什么**高见**? [3]

E: We think that "1+2" is definitely better than "2+2". It saves students from paying a year worth of tuition, which would **otherwise** cripple many less wealthy families and frighten them off. [4] Moreover, four years will be too long for a diploma program. As I understand it, a lot of Sino-British university cooperation undertake "1+2" or even "1+1".

C: 确实,"1+2"能帮助学生既省钱又省时间。但是只用一年的时间准备出国,学生能应付得来吗?学生是否会匆匆准备而去到英国后不适应?

E: That's why we require that 50% of the courses taken in China should be taught by our own staff and the remaining half by your faculty members. We think this is best for preparing students in language, learning behaviours, knowing British customs, and many other things.

C: 说到外国师资的问题,许多学生家长很关心师资情况,能否简要介绍一下贵校的师资情况?

E: The strength of the program takes root from our teaching team. We have highly motivated and qualified teachers aware that we are an educational institute where the knowledge given to our students will have an impact on their future. [5]

C: 贵校的英语老师和商务专业老师的情况如何?因为这是我们最关心的两方面。

E: All our English teachers are required to have teaching experience. They are all willing to assist students in their learning experience. Concerning the business side of our program, teachers are required not only to have teaching background but at least four years work experience.

C: 好的!贵校师资实力有保证,我们就放心推行"1+2"的方案。

E: Excellent! Shall we leave other details for another meeting? I guess that's quite fruitful for today.

Dialogue 2

Scenario: A Journalist (C) Is Interviewing a British Representative (B) in the Overseas Study Exhibition for More Information about the Advantage to Go to U.K.

C: 在那么多国家中,我们为什么要选择在英国学英语呢?

B: Studying English in the UK is the perfect opportunity to learn about UK life and culture **as** UK is home of the English language. [1] The language skills you will gain should set you on the path for future success, wherever and whatever that may be.

C: 英国教育有着什么样优势以吸引更多的留学生?

Chapter 10 Cooperation Talks 国际合作

B: The UK's tradition of education dates back hundreds of years and is constantly evolving. UK qualifications are recognised and respected throughout the world and by studying in the UK you will be building a solid foundation for your future.

C: 你能描述一些英国学校的**概况**吗？［2］

B: UK schools and colleges **provide** a vibrant, creative and challenging environment in which to learn and develop your potential and their standards are among the best in the world. ［3］ They continually have to prove that their courses meet strict criteria, with many other countries now trying to follow the standards set by the UK.

C: 英国的学习文化怎样？你可以勾勒一下在英国学习的情况吗？

B: Sure! You'll be putting your English language skills into practice every day, not only through your studies, but by using your English in everyday life, through film and television, newspapers and books, shopping and entertainment. All parts of the UK are English speaking. There are different regional accents throughout the UK, which may be different to English you have already heard, but you should soon adjust to it.

C: 英国的学术氛围都是世界有名的，那么大学的课外活动是不是也同样精彩呢？

B: Many schools and colleges will give you access to all sorts of leisure and social activities. There will be the opportunity to join sports teams, volunteer organisations and groups with specialist interests, such as drama, music, arts or the environment. Trips to local theatres, museums, tourist and sporting attractions as well as other places of interest are often also arranged.

C: 在英国求学，学费会很贵吗？现在的家长都比较关注**性价比**，他们倾向于选择澳洲、新西兰甚至法国等国家。［4］

B: The UK is home to the English language, a place with incredible heritage, an amazingly varied culture, and a fantastic social scene. You'll be learning more and more about the UK's diverse culture as you go, making friends and experiencing things you'll always remember. I admit that tuition in UK is a bit higher, but it's worth the price and you will find the invaluable essence of long and authentic British culture behind that.

联络口译

C: 现在英镑兑人民币比以前要低,那么英国方面是不是会加收学费呢?**加收的幅度会有多大呢?** [5]

B: There will be a slight increase to the tuition, but I am sure that Chinese parents and students will be able to afford that. With the appreciation of RMB, I believe that the living cost of overseas students in U.K. will be lower, so they don't have to worry about the tuition issues too much.

C: 有报道指出,现在英国学校吸收的外国留学生越来越多,英国方面会不会因学生数量增多而无暇顾及教学质量?你本人会不会有这方面的担心呢?

B: We shall never compromise quality for anything. British universities are renowned by their excellent tradition of teaching quality and research capacity. Even though more and more students are coming to U.K., we still set a bar for them and we shall not lower the bar simply because we want more headcounts.

Dialogue 3

Scenario: *An International Journalist (J) Is Interviewing a Representative from Ministry of Education of China (R) about the Well-being of Confucius Institutes in the World.*

J: What is the mission of Confucius Institute?

R: 孔子学院是非营利性语言推广机构,其宗旨是增进世界人民对中国语言和文化的了解,发展中国和外国的友好关系,促进世界多元文化发展,为构建和谐世界贡献力量。

J: Could you share some figures about Confucius Institutes? For example, how many of them are already functioning and how many of them are still in preparation?

R: 截至2007年,全球已经建立孔子学院,包括孔子课堂210所,分布在64个国家和地区。已经开班办学的有125所,其余85所都在抓紧筹办之中。

J: In the Beijing Confucius Institute headquarter, what are the regular working responsibilities?

R: 一是制订一系列的规章制度。二是在中方院长和教师的选派工作中,坚持严格把关、保证质量。三是积极组织编辑、出版和推广使用多种语言的教材和多媒体教学资源。四是开发并推出汉语考试的新品种,改进命题和考务。五是努力筹措资金,进一步加大中方对孔子学院的经费投入,2006年的总投入达到了2600多万美元。

Chapter 10 Cooperation Talks 国际合作

J: What are the **unique styles of running** Confucius Institute? [1]

R: 我们有几方面的举措。首先要面向社区开展非学历的汉语教学。然后，发挥带动作用，推动中小学开展汉语教学。**更重要的是开展学历教育，在教育中开设中国文化特色课程**，举办丰富多彩的文化活动。[2]

J: We are very interested in the classes featuring Chinese culture. Could you cite a few examples in this regards?

R: 我们主要**根据**当地社区的兴趣开设各种各样的课程，如：中医养生课、武术课、太极拳、少林拳、京剧，甚至北京奥运会的介绍也颇受欢迎。[3]

J: Could you tell us Confucius Institute is typically attracted to what kinds of people?

R: 公务员、公司职员、退休职员、司机、导游、学生和经商人员。他们或出于个人对中国文化的兴趣，或出于个人工作的需要来孔子学院求学。

J: **Could you cite some examples to show that Chinese involvement in the Confucius Institute is a cooperation program of mutual benefits**? [4]

R: 北京外国语大学先后派出系主任、骨干教师和志愿者25人赴9个国家11所大学开办孔子学院，既支持了外国办学，又使本校非英语专业师生得到了实地语言训练。罗马大学孔子学院还为北外选派了拉丁语教师。

J: What new features will the Confucius Institute represent for its betterment?

R: 今后孔子学院应建成"三个中心"，即推广中心、教学和培训中心、考试和研究中心，**以此**带动和引领当地社会学习汉语，使人们了解中国的热情持续高涨。[5]

IV. Notes for Interpreting

Dialogue 1

[1] 英国大学校长职位一般有 chancellor, vice chancellor 和 pro-vice-chancellor 三种。Chancellor 是"名誉校长"，vice chancellor 是真正的"校长"，pro-vice-chancellor 是"副校长"。因此本句里面，"巴顿校长"可译为 vice chancellor Pattern.

[2] 这句话比较长，如果完全照搬到汉语里面会让听众难以分清各部分关系。因此，在译文中，先概括"用两种选择"然后再分译 either... or... 的两部分。这样处理会让听众更容易把握句子的意思。联络口译的要旨是要促

联络口译

进双方交流，因此，适当变通句型是口译员应时刻注意的。

[3] "贵方有什么高见"，是中文里面的客套话，如果只译成 What do you have in your mind？或 What do you think of it？就显得不够体面。因此可以用 insight 一词来对译"高见"，于是本句就可以译为 I am looking forward to your insights.

[4] otherwise 在这里是"in other aspects, ways"的意思，指要是多交了一年的学费就会……

[5] 本句话比较长，在口译成汉语的时候，可以考虑使用断句的技巧，在定语从句的地方断开，然后补上主语"他们"另起一句。

Dialogue 2

[1] as… 是"因为"的意思。根据汉语语序"前因后果"的习惯，如果我们在口译时调整顺序把 as 后面的内容放在前面，那么就没有必要加上"因为"二字。当然，如果按着原来的顺序翻译的话，就要加上"因为"二字。

[2] 概况一词可用 overview，general picture，而另外比较常用的词是 landscape。译者可根据需要选择不同的词语。

[3] 在对话中，不必过分着眼于 provide 一词。如果把"提供"放到句子里面，使用"提供丰富多彩、创新和挑战的环境"这一句型，中间的定语部分就会稍长。现在用"气氛"作为主语，省去"提供"，会让句子更为精简。

[4] "性价比"原意应为 price-to-performance ratio，但是如果直接用这一翻译，那么就会显得不符合交谈的对象，因为现在谈及的是学校，不是某一种产品。所以，在这里处理成 tuition-and-quality balance 或者 tuition-to-quality ratio。

[5] "加收的幅度会有多大"看似简单，但是要在翻译中用比较好的句型来表达却不容易。这里用了"how much will the British schools bring the tuition up"来对译。how much 表示幅度，bring up 表示加收。类似地，如果要表示减少的幅度，那么把 up 改为 down 就可以了。

Dialogue 3

[1] unique style of running… 直译就是"经营……的独特风格"，在这里不妨译为"办学特色"让听众更容易掌握。

[2] "更重要的是开展学历教育，在教育中开设中国文化特色课程……"汉语行文不怕重复，但是英语很少会重复。因此，口译此句时如果把后半部分另起一句，就要重复 in the education，显得累赘。解决办法是使用定语从句，用 where 引导，那么口译出来的英文就简练了。

Chapter 10　Cooperation Talks 国际合作

［3］"根据当地社区的兴趣开设各种各样的课程"，不要一听到"根据……"就马上说 according to... 我们还有更好的词组可选择，如 tailor... to... 或者 intended for...

［4］如果照英文的语序译，"你能否举些例子来说明一下中方参与到孔子学院是一项互惠互利的合作项目"，那么汉语译文的宾语部分显得较长，这样听众听的时候会费劲，所以译员可以调整顺序，先说长宾语部分，再说"你能否举些例子来说明这一点"。

［5］如果看到"以此……"就用 in order to/ so as to 的句型，那么这句话的英译就太长了。所以我们可以在这里断句，用"This will enable... to..."的句型来代替。

Chapter 11 Dealing with Cultural Differences
文化差异处理
口译主题：文化交流

I. Liaison Interpreting Tips

Cultural communication/exchange is a broad category for the events related to films, movies, dramas, journalism, arts, mass media and so on. One must be noted that cultural communication in this chapter is perceived from a "grass root" perspective, instead of the policy level or the official level. This, however, does not make the interpreting task any easier, because interpreters are supposed to know the genres of the activities and some jargons in the artistic criticism language (examples like structuralism, post-modernism, constructivism, de-constructivism, motif, etc.).

The difficulty of interpreting for the cultural events is compounded by various quotations that speakers occasionally refer to. Quotations possibly are several lines from a certain film, recent remarks from a celebrity, statement or announcement of an entertainment company, or even original lines and stanzas in the literary works. If, fortunately, the interpreter happens to know the exact translation of the quotation (e.g. "What's in a name? That which we call a rose by any other name would smell as sweet."), credits would be added to the interpreter. If the quotation is strange and new to the interpreter, one coping tactic for this unexpected quotation bomb is to paraphrase the meaning of the quoted sentence(s). For example, interpreters may say "名字与什么有关系呢？就算把玫瑰花叫做别的名字，它还是照样芳香。" Of course, a more concise and polished interpretation would be "名称与什么有关系呢？玫瑰不叫玫瑰，依然芳香如故"。

As cultural activities sometimes beget extreme idealism and expression of individual thoughts, interpreters may be put into an embarrassing position, where they cannot see

Chapter 11　Dealing with Cultural Differences 文化差异处理

eye to eye with the speakers. Given this situation, chances are that interpreters may engage in mental argument rather than listening attentively. At this point, interpreters should remind themselves to steer away from the personal bias and listen carefully. What's more important, they should interpret the statements convincingly, without additional personal undertone.

Because of the varieties and ever changing nature of cultural events, updated news about cultural activities should be constantly followed by interpreters. One worthy program in this regard is Cultural Express in CCTV 9 (Air time: Monday to Sunday Beijing Time: 2:30, 8:30, 14:30, 20:30. It is also accessible via Internet at http://www.cctv.com/program/cultureexpress/01/index.shtml), which is a featured program dedicated to any cultural events taken place home and abroad. Students and beginners in interpretation may feel free to watch the program and pick up the names of the celebrities, movie titles, jargons of critique and so on.

Ⅱ. Task-based Preparation

1. Useful Expressions

赢得青睐　appeal to
screen writer　编剧
《失控陪审团》　*Runaway Jury*
blockbuster　大片
默契　chemistry

莎士比亚剧团　Shakespeare Play Groups
to stifle its essence　扼杀了精粹
small cast　小剧团/为数不多的演员
"less is more"　越不繁，越不凡/少既
　是多

Elizabethan audience　伊丽莎白时代的
　观众
巡回演出　round tour show
风靡全球　appeal to the world audience

美术组　fine art group
工头　manual workers/errand runners
招待所　hostel/guesthouse
圈内　within the circle
tuck your tail　夹着尾巴做人
受不了这个气　can/could not bear it

2. Interpreting Formulas

[1] We want our characters to stand up to the very high expectations that viewers have when watching...　在观看……的时候，我们希望我们的角色能达到观众的期望。

[2] How will you keep this film from becoming a formula driven plot-based one like... 你怎样避免这部电影沦为公式化的情节剧，如……

[3] By the time we started shooting the whole film, they had really developed this chemistry that was a surprise and a delight to all of us. 到我们开拍整部电影的时候，他们已经默契，我们对此又惊又喜！

[4] What does TNT do to deliver a Shakespearean play in a way Shakespeare would have intended it? 那么TNT剧团在还原莎剧本来面目，或者说上演原汁原味的莎剧方面有什么样的举措？

[5] The plays were after all written to be performed with limited scenery which calls upon the imagination of the audience, live music, small casts, energetic physical performances and a sensitivity to poetry. 剧本都适合在有限的场景上演，能焕发出观众的想象力，还有生动的音乐、为数不多的演员、激情洋溢的表演和诗意般的触角。

[6] Why does TNT once again choose Shanghai as the first destination of the China round tour show? 在这次中国巡回演出，TNT剧团为什么会再次选择上海作为第一站上演莎士比亚的戏剧呢？

[7] What is it about Shakespeare that is timeless and relevant till today? Why do his plays continue to appeal to the world audience? 莎士比亚的永恒性和现代性是怎样体现出来的？为什么至今还风靡全球？

[8] When did you begin to direct a film? Was it successful? 你什么时候开始做导演的？你执导的第一部影片成功吗？

[9] Did you try to get used to being wronged, keeping a low profile or even tucking your tail? 是否要善于受委屈，为人低调，夹着尾巴做人？

[10] China's market-based economy is developing on the right track, but the cultural circle is still lagging behind. 我们这个国家在走入市场经济之后，一直沿着正确的方向在发展，但是文化领域却是滞后的。

III. Liaison Interpreting Practice

Dialogue 1

Scenario: A Reporter (R) from a Chinese Media Magazine Is Interviewing the Director and Producer (D) of GIO, a Studio for an Upcoming Movie.

R: GIO制作室前两部电影因刻画了强悍、复杂的女性冲突而大热，此次拍摄本电影，会不会着力描写女性形象，希望再受女性观众的青睐？

Chapter 11 Dealing with Cultural Differences 文化差异处理

D: GIO has taken it to a higher level on characters regardless of gender. So naturally we want our characters to stand up to the very high expectations that viewers have when watching GIO. Our screen writers did a remarkable job conjuring them, but our actors really took each character and gave them life, humanity and complexity.

R: GIO 制作的其他电影因质量而获奖不少，这会不会给你带来压力呢？[1]

D: Well, I've never been one to worry about awards and such, but we do feel the pressure of wanting to make the best film we can possibly make. For most of us working on the film, this is a passion project, so we give it our all on this film.

R: 你怎样避免这部电影沦为公式化的情节剧，如《失控陪审团》？您打算采用以人物刻画为主的剧情来**吸引**观众吗？[2]

D: I think if we continue to stay true to our passion and what we're trying to accomplish, I think we'll be fine. As I've said, this isn't just a job for most of us, but a real passion.

R: 你是知名的大片制作人。你有没有想过发展与影片相关的产品？建立网络和创造网上游戏会不会是计划的一部分呢？

D: You know, it's all just about story-telling, regardless of if you do it in a movie theater, on television, comic book, video game, on mobile phones or the Internet. [3] Each has its own challenges, but at the end of the day, it's always about a group of characters going on a journey. If you tell that right, it's always rewarding, irrespective of the medium you're working in.

R: 你希望网上游戏会怎样影响观众？

D: We're hopeful that by playing the game they can get into the head space that our characters have to live in. Perhaps these viewers will gain a unique perspective on how and why the characters do what they do.

R: 你在拍摄过程中怎样让剧组找到**默契**和**协调**各自的关系？[4]

D: The chemistry grew **organically** by itself. [5] When we went abroad to shoot some scenes, the actors ended up spending a lot of time together off camera, back at the hotel, out to dinner, after work... and they bonded in a way we couldn't have predicted. By the time we started shooting the whole film, they had really developed this chemistry that was a surprise and a delight to all of us.

联络口译

Dialogue 2

Scenario: *A British Shakespeare Play Group, TNT, Is Going to Put on Tour Play around China. They Come to Shanghai as the First Stop and Their Director (D) Is Interviewed by a Local Journalist (J).*

J: TNT 剧团与其他莎士比亚剧团相比有什么不同呢?

D: All too often, Shakespeare suffers from the hands of directors and even designers imposing an interpretation on the original that stifles its essence. TNT works carefully to bring out the true richness and depth of Shakespeare. This approach has been much appreciated by a wide audience **who is often surprised at how accessible and relevant** Shakespeare's plays become when they are performed in the manner Shakespeare might have intended. [1]

J: 那么 TNT 剧团在还原莎剧本来面目,或者说**上演原汁原味的莎剧**方面有什么的举措? [2]

D: The plays were after all written to be performed with limited scenery which calls upon the imagination of the audience, live music, small casts, energetic physical performances and a sensitivity to poetry. All of these elements are present in a TNT Shakespeare production. **Less is more!** [3]

J: 在 21 世纪的今天,我们为什么要上演原汁原味的莎剧呢?

D: It's important to rescue Shakespeare from his admirers and get back to what he intended: fast, fluid, dynamic theatre without complicated scene changes, big casts, realistic settings. It works because that is how it is supposed to work.

J: 你觉得当代观众在观看莎剧的时候最需要什么?观众在观看之前要做什么准备吗? [4]

D: Imagination is crucial. The great thing about the Elizabethan audience, back then, was that they were prepared to use their imagination. Our modern media, sadly, takes away the imagination of the public and we try to return that real thrill to them. If audiences want to enjoy Shakespearean plays, they had better bring their imagination with them and be prepared to visualize along the poetic lines of the plays.

J: 在这次的中国巡回演出,TNT 剧团为什么会再次选择上海作为第一站上演莎士比亚的戏剧呢?是不是看中上海观众的热情和慷慨?

Chapter 11　Dealing with Cultural Differences 文化差异处理

D: I would like to say that we are back in Shanghai because of the audience—we have had a great response from public and students over the last years and we really appreciate the lively and intelligent audience in your city. We offer them all we can and hope we and they will be rewarded with a moving, exciting and even comic evening of great romance.

J: 最后，我想问的是，莎士比亚的**永恒性和现代性**是怎样体现出来的？为什么至今还风靡全球？［5］

D: The answer is simple. Shakespeare belongs to all the humanities, transcending the time and place to reach into the hearts of viewers. His plays represent the eternal themes of human societies and thus touch the souls of us all.

Dialogue 3

Scenario: *A Chinese Film Director (D) Is Interviewed by a Foreign Reporter (R) in an International Film Exhibition about His Career.*

R: What was your dream when you were still a kid?

D: 我小时候的梦想是当画家。我从小学画到中学，一直在学校的美术组。每次走过电影院，我特别羡慕站在架子上画电影海报的人，我特别想成为一个专业的画电影海报的人。

R: Why did you turn out to be a screen writer later?

D: 在一个摄制组里，美工在我看来**别人就拿你当一工头**：你把这桌子、椅子都搬出去，咱们要那种沙发，你们搬过来！［1］编剧就不一样了，制片人、导演很重视剧本。那个时候，编剧是拿稿费，收入比摄影师、美术师要高得多。［2］天长日久，在剧组待久了，认识了组内的一些编剧以后，我就开始写剧本了。

R: Was it easy to swap from a screen writer to a director?

D: 非常不容易。不可能你一来别人就相信你，就把一个组交给你，那么多钱让你管。那时导演是由单位领导来指派，所以你首先要满足电影学院导演系毕业的人。但对他们而言，你却是业余的。但作为一名编剧没有人去管你，你自己愿意写，回家写去吧。你投稿给电视剧制作中心、电影厂文学部，他们说可以拍了，这时候就会给你在招待所租个房间，请你修改。

R: When did you begin to direct a film? Was it successful?
D: 我独立执导的第一个片子是1997年,那时候给我的资金也不多,但是我觉得自己很幸运,那部片子很成功!

R: Is it difficult to get into the film circle in China?
D: 初入行的人,**比较在乎**圈内前辈的认可,但慢慢你就会发现,其实圈内的评价不重要,更重要的是观众对你的认可。[3]

R: How about you? Was it difficult for you to get into the circle? What efforts have you made? Did you try to get used to **being wronged, keeping a low profile or even tucking your tail**? [4]
D: 当然更重要的还是自己的坚持和努力,这么多年走过来,肯定是有很多的挫折、关卡。在面对挫折时,有些人就会容易灰心,丧失信心:我不干了!他受不了这个气,我是可以受委屈的人。遇到对我不公正的时候,有挫败感的时候,我还是能够迅速地调整自己。我开始时会有点儿生气,但更多的是脑子里想,你等着瞧,我一定会把这事给做成的。

R: What kind of dreams do you cherish as a director?
D: 我觉得中国电影的题材和风格可以更宽泛一点,更多样一点。我们这个国家在走入市场经济之后,一直沿着正确的方向在发展,但是经济起来了,文化领域却是滞后的 [5]。我希望文化领域能够加速发展,思想开放一些。这对我来说是一个梦想。

R: How do you think of the positive and negative movies?
D: 我承认,积极是好的,但这并不意味着消极都是不好的。当你来拍一个电影,让别人了解、认识这个民族的时候,他可能是用这民族的灾难,让你更深刻地认识到这个民族。它的方式不见得是积极的,但是从更大的意义上来说它是积极的。

Ⅳ. Notes for Interpreting

Dialogue 1

[1] 本句话可以顺着译:"GIO films have won many awards for their qualities, do you feel pressure?"但是这样译,意思还不是很清楚,所以可以把顺序倒过

Chapter 11　Dealing with Cultural Differences 文化差异处理

来,"Do you feel pressure to achieve/live up to the qualities and awards that other GIO films have received"?

［2］"吸引观众"当然可以译为 attract the viewers,但是还有另外一个很好的词可以用就是 intrigue,这个词有"引人入胜"的意思。

［3］这个句子列举的项目比较多。在真正场合中,由于说话人语速较快或其他原因不能记住这五项时,可以用省略及概括的技巧,把该句翻译成:"不管是在电影、电视、漫画书、游戏、手机或网络上"。这样的话意思不会受损。

［4］默契可以翻译为 chemistry,而协调各自的关系不一定要翻译为 coordinate each other,用 balance 一词也可以,因为 balance 有协调平衡各方面关系的意思。

［5］organically 有 characterized by continuous or natural development 的意思,不一定指有机体增长,所以翻译成"自生自发"为好。

Dialogue 2

［1］who is often surprised at how accessible and relevant 如果直译的话是:"通常为可接触和有关系而惊讶",这样翻译没有把意思说清楚,这句话其实是说这样的莎剧更接近观众,所以我们可以用"不再遥不可及"来翻译。

［2］在本句话中,提问的人在中间部分更改了措辞,把"还原莎剧本来面目"改为"上演原汁原味的莎剧"。在口译的时候,译员一般没有必要把这种更改或重复的信息译出,除非发言人重复信息是为了强调。因此,本句只译 deliver a Shakespearean play in a way Shakespeare would have intended it 就可以了。

［3］Less is more 是一句经常引用的名言。字面意思是"少即多"。在这个采访的场合,我们要根据发言人的身份来考虑一下译文。因为这句话是一名导演说出的,所以口译的时候尽量把这句话译得文雅或有修辞效果。我们可译为:"过犹不及"或者"越不繁,越不凡"。

［4］在口译"观众在观看之前要做什么准备吗?"一句时,为了使译文译得更地道,我们可以加入插入语的成分。如:What preparation, *if any*, should audience make before they go to watch the play? 或者可以译为:Is it necessary to make some preparation before they go to the show? *If so*, what can they get prepared?

［5］"永恒性和现代性"是抽象名语,当然在英语里有 eternity 和 modernity 相对应,但是如果不想把译文弄得学究气息太浓,我们也可以用形容词 timeless and relevant till today 来表示这一意思。

Dialogue 3

［1］ "别人就拿你当一工头"可有两层含义的理解。一是身份上被人看低，二是工作中常被人使唤干活。所以口译的时候除了把第一层意思 artists are merely manual workers 口译出来外，还需要把第二层意思 They are bossed around and asked to run errands like... 翻译出来。

［2］ "收入多得多"当然可以说：earn more than... 但是用 out-earn 一词更生动、简洁。在联络口译的时候我们可以注意这些简洁的表达方式。如：甲比乙重…… A outweighs B by...；甲比乙表现得更好 A outperforms B。

［3］ "比较在乎"这里所表达的意思是"更倾向于在乎……"所以，我们可以用 tend to... 或 be inclined to... 的词组来翻译。

［4］ be wronged 的意思是被人误会或错怪，所以可以译为受委屈；keep a low profile/keep a low key 的意思是为人低调、保持低调或不张扬；tuck one's tail 的意思是 humble oneself，即中文的"夹着尾巴做人"。

［5］ 如果把这句话的每个分句都译（After China entered into the market-based economy, it is developing along the right path; even though the economy is developing, the cultural circle is lagging.），这样译文显得松散而冗长，不够简洁，不利于双方交流。因此，我们把意思重复的部分省略（China's market-based economy is developing on the right track, but the cultural circle is still lagging behind.）。

Chapter 12　Sports Interpreting　体育口译

口译主题：体育活动

Ⅰ. Liaison Interpreting Tips

Interpreting for sport events is quite challenging, especially for budding interpreters, because the task requires the mastery of various jargons, slangs, names of the players and the clubs they work for and many more.

The threat of sport interpreting arises from the specific jargons in each and every kind of sport. The number of the jargons ranges from a dozen to several hundreds. For example, in golfing, the name for each golfing club, shot and swing is unique. Even if you are mastery in golfing, you may not be familiar with those expressions in other sports. Another handy example is the basketball. If you are to interpret for the NBA events, you are supposed to remember the name(s) of the team(s) and also every player in the team(s) and their corresponding positions, let alone their coaches' name, the technical tactics they are used to, the former famous players in the history, and the potential players they are expected to acquire from or trade with other teams. The list can be on and on. To be a good interpreter in sports, one must be an expert or a fanatic fan for sports. This requires months or even years of involvement in the particular sport. If interpreters are less crazy about sports and are assigned to serve as an interpreter for a certain event, preparation has to be as exhaustive as possible. It is advisable that interpreters require a name list of players and coaches and research into their history and recent developments.

For the ease of accessing some (if not all) jargons of sports, interpreters are advised to browse the following websites for reference：
1. ESPN：This is a very comprehensive website for sports fans. It is updated on daily basis and almost every sport is followed. For Chinese version, please go to http：//

www.espnstar.com.cn/; for English, please go to http://www.espnstar.com/.

2. NBA: For basketball fans and interpreters for basketball events, this is a must-visit website. The English version is at http://www.nba.com/, while the Chinese version is at http://www.nba.tom.com/.

3. PGA: This is an official website of Professional Golfers Association. You may access at http://www.pga.info/ and find out the latest news and upcoming events in the golfing community.

4. BBC Sports at http://www.news.bbc.co.uk/sport. On the left side of the webpage, you can locate "A-Z of sports" and you can click any sport you like and there will be a specific webpage for that sport.

One final tip for interpreters is the dressing code of the event. As sporting activities usually imply less formal dress, interpreters must ask the event organization authority for the dressing code beforehand. Otherwise, it would be a bit strange for a dressed up interpreter to be around a group of casual wear players. Of course, formal dress is required for certain events, such as press conference and official receptions. Again, that is why it is important that interpreters inquire about the dressing code ahead of time.

II. Task-based Preparation

1. Useful Expressions

Athens　雅典
悉尼奥运　Sydney Olympics
四分之一决赛　quarterfinal
fare better　更上一层楼／做得更好

110 meter hurdles final　110米跨栏决赛
超自然　surreal
田径　track and filed
为……争了口气　bring credits to…
follow your lead　追随你的步伐
我的本行是……　what I am good at is…

Chapter 12 Sports Interpreting 体育口译

in want of   缺乏

合同年限   contract term

start from scratch   从零开始

raise the bar   提高标准

大人物   well-known figure / big fish

a dark horse   黑马

2. Interpreting Formulas

[1] What do you like about China's team going into the Olympics?   您觉得中国队参加奥运比赛会有怎样的成绩?

[2] We got into the quarterfinal. We had some success, but also some tough times.   我们挺进了四分之一决赛,取得了一定的成功,但也经历了一些创伤。

[3] Do you expect more Chinese players to make it to the NBA?   您觉得会有更多的篮球运动员加盟 NBA 吗?

[4] Until then, there had never been an Asian in the final of that event in the Olympics, so that was already an accomplishment.   在那时候,从来没有一个亚洲运动员能跻身奥运会的决赛,所以我觉得自己已经取得了成功。

[5] Your win has influenced another generation of young athletes in China to follow your lead.   您的胜出影响到下一代的中国运动员来追随您的步伐。

[6] Do you think that you will ever top that feeling of winning that gold medal?   您觉得会有什么比赢得金牌更胜一筹吗?

[7] Our club is in good shape and quite strong.   俱乐部已经粗具规模,也有一些有实力的球员。

[8] Now given that you are in charge of a completely newly-built team, do you feel any pressure?   现在要执教一支还完全是新组建的俱乐部,您有压力吗?

[9] I will also enlist some of the sound players whom I coached before.   我以前所带的一些不错的球员也在考虑之列。

[10] 您在国际足坛上可算是大人物,现在来到中国的地方俱乐部执教会不会感到委屈?   You are a well-known figure in the international football community. Now you are to coach a Chinese local team. Has it occurred to you that you are a big fish in a small pool?

联络口译

III. Liaison Interpreting Practice

Dialogue 1

Scenario: *A Journalist (J) from a New York Based Sport Magazine Is Interviewing a Famous Chinese Basketball Player (P), Who Is Serving for an American Basketball League and Is about to Return to China for the 2008 Olympic Games.*

J: What do you like about China's team going into the Olympics?

P: 中国队已经参加了一次奥运会、一次世锦赛,已取得了一定的经验。像他们这个年龄的运动员,能有这些经历是为数不多的。而且他们一直都在进步。我觉得我们在自家门前参加奥运比赛获胜的机会更大。

J: How was your Olympic experience **in Athens** different than your experience **in Sydney**? [1]

P: 首先,悉尼奥运会是我首次参加奥运会比赛。我当时十分兴奋能成为其中的一员。所以很自然,我更多的是感到兴奋而不是压力。我那时20岁而且是队中最年轻的队员,所以我要做的就是在赛场上往前冲。在雅典奥运会,虽然我也很兴奋,但是更多的却是压力。我带领整个队伍,挺进了四分之一决赛,取得了一定的成功,但也经历了一些创伤。

J: Do you expect your team to **fare better** than in Beijing? [2]

P: 我当然希望如此。我们也应如此。

J: Does playing in the NBA and for the Chinese national team mean anything special to you?

P: 能在世界上最好的球队打比赛对我而言有极大的意义,可以帮助我提升技能和经验。同时我也会效力国家队,希望能帮助国家队变得更好、更强大。

J: **Do you expect** that the **fans** will be crazy about your team at the Olympics? [3]

P: 球迷一直都给予我们帮助。篮球在中国十分流行,很多球迷都喜欢打篮球,也喜欢看比赛。只要跟国家队有关的事情,他们都会从报上、电视上获知,他们对我们十分关心。[4]

J: Why do you think basketball is such a popular sport in China?

Chapter 12　Sports Interpreting 体育口译

P：因为篮球有趣啊！大家都很喜欢打篮球,真的很喜欢！［5］

J：Do you expect more Chinese players to make it to the NBA?
P：也许每五年有一名吧,这也说不准。

Dialogue 2

Scenario：*A Foreign Reporter (R) Is Interviewing a Chinese Athlete (A), Who Has Just Won the Olympic Gold Medal.*

R：That moment when you're lining up to start the 110 meter hurdles final, what was going through you mind?
A：说实话,我头脑一片空白,我没想啥,我知道自己会有所突破。在那时候,从来没有一个亚洲运动员能够跻身奥运会的决赛,所以我觉得自己已经取得了成功。我只是想做好自己,尽最大努力去跑,我想的就是那些。

R：That moment when you crossed the finishing line and you realized you'd won. What was the feeling?
A：就像刚才我说的那样,那时我脑子一片空白。我赢了,感到一切事物都是**超现实的**［1］。我很难形容,就像腾云驾雾一般,所说的话语,所做出的动作,……好像都不是我自己的。就好像我正旁观着有人在做这些事情,在说这些事情。因为太幸福,太兴奋。正在发生的一切事情,我都难以接受,仿佛乾坤颠倒了。

R：**You say the world had turned upside down, well, it certainly turned upside down for athletics**, you'd broken through the barrier, and an Asian man had won a major sprint event at the Olympics. How do you make sense of that? How do you realize the historical importance of that? ［2］
A：意义很大,因为过去欧洲人和美洲人总以为亚洲人在田径赛事上不行,对他们不能构成威胁,在男子项目上尤其如此。而我们也常以为自己是中国人,田径不是咱家的强项。所以我赢了比赛,为亚洲运动员争了口气。

R：Do you think that your win has influenced another generation of young athletes in China to follow your lead?

89

A: 我的胜出希望可以给其他人带来鼓舞,告诉他们不管面对什么障碍、什么困难,都要努力**直面挑战**。[3] 挑战是要我们勇于面对的,我们也能克服挑战。每个人都能做到。

R: How much sacrifice do you have to give? How much dedication is needed to achieve that gold?

A: 说实话,训练是非常辛苦的。不过习惯了,就好了。你要竭尽全力,做到最好[4],因为这是自己的职业。我觉得自己能拿到奥运会金牌十分幸运。

R: It's been said that winning a gold medal is like winning a million dollars, that the sponsorships make you a wealthy man. So do you expect to be a rich man soon?

A: 在生活中,我常常认为精神满足高于物质满足,更别谈情感满足了。这是我的真实想法。如果一个人有太多的钱,那么钱仅是一个数字。其实很简单,如果你表现出色,取得了好的结果,你会得到褒奖,这就是通行的法则。此时此刻,在我的同伴中间,我认为自己是个富人了,但我一直认为精神财富远比物质财富重要。

R: Taking about material life, it's also said that you enjoy **singing karaoke** — you're quite good at it. Would you like to sing, perhaps make a record at some time? [5]

A: 当我想放松的时候,我就会跟亲朋好友一起唱K,但只是为了娱乐。我唱歌水平只是停留在业余级别。我绝对不适合在公众面前唱歌,唱歌不是我的本行,我的本行是跑步。

R: Finally, do you think that you will ever top that feeling of winning that gold medal? Do you think anything in your life will ever compare to that in the future?

A: 我相信肯定会有更好的东西,生活是难以预料的。我不知道我退休后会怎样,只要我还有梦想,我都会努力实现自己的梦想。

Dialogue 3

Scenario: An International Coach Mr. Stone (S) Is Hired for a Chinese Local Football Team and Is Now Receiving an Interview with a Local Newspaper Reporter (R).

Chapter 12　Sports Interpreting 体育口译

R：铁山足球俱乐部对于大家都很陌生，**司通教练**能介绍一下这家俱乐部吗？[1]

S：Our team is not yet present in the national competition. But our club is in good shape and quite strong. As the Chinese national competition is very competitive, we are in want of more players, especially strong players for an even better team.

R：司通教练能透露一下您的教练班子将怎么成立吗？**您的合同年限和待遇又是多少**？[2]

S：Mr. Sharon will come here to join me. He was my assistant when we were in France, so we are quite familiar with each other. Still, we shall look for some other coaching members. This is my first time to coach a local team in China. I have to explore and know my team bit by bit.

R：司通教练您有很多成功的经验，每执教一支球队都非常成功，现在执教一支还完全是新组建的俱乐部，您有压力吗？

S：Although I have lots of successful experiences, yet I actually start from scratch when we are talking about the Chinese football national competition. This is my first time in a Chinese club. I hope my friends and colleagues will work with me, **to raise the bar** of the national competition. [3] I am looking forward to my work.

R：为什么会选择来中国执教呢？

S：Reasons are tow-fold. First of all, I feel that there is a great room for improvement in Chinese football, and I would like to do my bit to the well-being of Chinese football. Secondly, I want to enrich my coaching experience. As I have coached in Europe and Americas, naturally I want to come to Asia. It so happened that Tieshan Club contacted me and here I am.

R：司通教练您在国际足坛上可算是大人物，现在来到中国的地方俱乐部执教会不会感到**委屈**？[4]

S：We all have our goals in life. I love football. I hope people's attention will be shifted from me to my coached team. As a matter of fact, China has favorable policies and investment in football. I am not at all in the small pool.

91

R：司通教练能评价一下铁山俱乐部吗？

S：Tieshan has a good foundation and is well-managed. I have great communication with the administrative guys and the players themselves. I believe that Tieshan will be a **dark horse** in the national competition. 〔5〕

R：请问铁山俱乐部会吸收什么样的球员来效力呢？

S：I shall extend my invitations to some of our desired players, like some of the domestic retired players. I shall include them in my team. In the meantime, I shall invite some international players to come to China. I will also enlist some of the sound players whom I coached before.

R：司通教练您说过您很喜欢中国，那么您喜欢中国的什么呢？

S：China of today is very open and tolerant. I feel privileged to live and work here. Chinese food is very famous among us. I love the enduring culture and history of China.

Ⅳ. Notes for Interpreting

Dialogue 1

〔1〕在双方都熟知的情况下说"雅典奥运会"、"悉尼奥运会"、"北京奥运会"时，可以只说 in Athens, Sydney, Beijing。这样翻译可以避免多次重复 Olympic Games。

〔2〕fare better 的意思是 perform better，因此翻译为"取得更佳成绩"或"有更优秀的表现"均可。

〔3〕采访某人时，一般会用 do you expect 开头，但并不一定要翻译为"你期待……"，因为在非正式文体中 I expect... 的意思是 indicate that one supposes something to be so but has no firm evidence or knowledge。所以翻译为"您觉得……"更为恰当。

〔4〕fans 一般会译为"……迷"，如 football fans "足球迷"，但是近几年"粉丝"的译法也较常见，所以可以根据场合而改变译法，如 fans of Yao Ming 译为"姚明的粉丝"就很恰当了。

〔5〕"因为篮球有趣啊！"这句话带有"不言自明"的语气，要把这个语气译出，在英语译文中最好增加 "..., you know" 这一短语。

Dialogue 2

〔1〕"超现实"在这里所表达的意思是"让人无法相信、神奇的"，而不是"超自然"

Chapter 12　Sports Interpreting 体育口译

的意思。所以要译为 surreal，而不是 supernatural。

［2］这个问题是建立在对前面一个问题回答"仿佛乾坤颠倒了"的基础上。译者如果没有成功译出这句话，后面的 You say the world had turned upside down, well it certainly turned upside down for athletics 就无从谈起了。所以在联络和陪同口译中，当双方多次提到同一样东西的时候，译员要固定用同一种翻译，如果译员变来变去的话，双方交谈就难以实现最佳的交谈效果。

［3］"直面……"可以译为 face... head on，因为 head on 词组就有迎面的意思，这样比翻译成 face... directly 更口语化，更符合联络口译的语体。

［4］"竭尽全力"当然可以译为 do one's utmost to... 或者是 try one's best to... 但是比较口语化的翻译也可以说 give what(ever) it takes。

［5］sing karaoke 光听英文是容易懂的，但是要变成中文，口译转换的时候需要思考一下，因为 karaoke 的中文翻译是"卡拉 OK"，不能完全算中文。其实很多情况下，中英之间不会有完全的对译，所以翻译成"唱 K"或"K 歌"就可以了，这些说法已广为接受。

Dialogue 3

［1］采访中，记者可以以"司通教练"开头作为尊称，但翻译成英文的时候，没有必要每次都译为 Coach Stone，而是直接用 You... 开头就可以了，因为这样更直接更亲切。如本句，如果译成"Could Coach Stone introduce this club to us"就显得比较正式。

［2］在中国的文化里面，工资、年龄、婚姻状况是可以讨论的，但是在西方文化中，这些是个人隐私，一般不会在公开场合讨论。所以，作为联络口译员有必要在传递信息的同时，把语气缓和一下。如本句中加了"if this is not an impertinent question"，"希望您不要介意"，"希望您不要觉得这问题是无礼的"，很明显感觉好多了。

［3］raise the bar 是"提高标准、提高水平"的意思。这一用法现在十分常见，当然 bring it to the next level 也有"提高水平"的意思。

［4］这里"委屈"的意思并不是"含冤、理亏"的意思，而是"大材小用"的意思，所以可以用一个生动的英语表达"big fish in a small pool"。

［5］dark horse 就是我们中文的"黑马"。这一词语已经不局限于体育活动，而是在其他领域被广泛地使用。但要注意与这一词语表达相近的另外一个习语 a black sheep，意思是 a member of a family or group who is regarded as a disgrace to it，中文则可以译为"害群之马"或"不肖子"。

Chapter 13 Diplomatic Interpreting
政治外交口译
口译主题：政治访问

I. Liaison Interpreting Tips

Liaison interpreting in the politics and diplomatic context is taking place constantly across China, with its endeavors of going global. Many university graduates will assume the position of liaison interpreters for local governments and various governing authorities and serve as in-house interpreters for the relevant bodies. The performance of the interpreters, therefore, has everything to do with the impression left upon the overseas guests. It is advisable that interpreters follow the head-ups listed bellow.

Sound delivery is very important, because it gives listeners the impression of reliability. Interpreters must be acutely aware of the presentation of their voices and avoid any potentially annoying noises (e. g. "um", "ah", "er", etc.), dragging tone, audible breath, prolonged silence, and unnaturally fast or slow pace of speech.

As far as the sentence structures are concerned, it is desirable that the delivery of the interpretation is free of false start (which means that interpreters cannot round up a sentence as a whole, stop in the middle of the sentence and start with another sentence), redundant sentence fillers and unjustified fragments.

As politics and diplomatic liaison interpreting usually takes place in formal venues and contexts, speech of formal register is thus frequently used. Interpreters should be able to choose words and phrases with formal register in addressing the audience.

Furthermore, in-house interpreters must be politically correct when interpreting. Alterations and adjustments are necessary if they are politically incorrect. For example,

Chapter 13　Diplomatic Interpreting 政治外交口译

foreign guests, out of their habitual behaviors, will juxtapose China, China Macau and Hong Kong. Interpreters in this case should render the remarks as "中国内地,中国澳门和中国香港"。

One final point is that interpreters must learn the titles of both parties present by heart. As the titles and naming habits vary from one country to another, interpreters are advised to check the titles and their ranking (or pecking order in seniority) with the guests. When interpreting, should/need be, interpreters may add a note of explanation to the hosts that "the position is equivalent to so and so in our country". For example, "Secretary of State for Education and Skills" in Chinese is "教育技能大臣". Interpreters may add that "相当于我国的部长级". This will help the listeners to get a clearer picture of the position.

For self-improvement purpose, interpreters may frequent the website of Ministry of Foreign Affairs of P. R. C. at http://www.mfa.gov.cn/chn/gxh/tyb/ where Chinese and English texts and news are available.

Ⅱ. Task-based Preparation

1. Useful Expressions

友好城市　twin cities / sister cities
pharmaceutical companies　制药公司
"新展馆、新展期、新机遇"　"New Complex, New Phase, New Opportunities"
at your earliest convenience　尽早

环境保护　environmental protection
气候变化　climate change
清洁能源　clean energy
strategic economic dialogue　战略经济对话
US-China Ten-Year Energy and Environment Cooperation Framework　《中美能源环境十年合作框架》
Copenhagen Climate Summit　哥本哈根气候峰会
减排　emission reduction
单位GDP能耗　energy consumption per unit GDP

温室气体　greenhouse gas（GHG）
compact fluorescent lamps　紧凑型荧光灯
incandescent lamps　白炽灯
better/higher gas mileage cars　节油汽车

泰国　Thailand
缅甸　Myanmar
老挝　Laos
柬埔寨　Cambodia
"信心之旅"　Journey of Confidence
中国证监会　China Securities Regulatory Commission
瑞士信贷　Credit Suisse
中立国　neutral country / neutral state
military pact　军事条约
NATO（North Atlantic Treaty Organization）　北大西洋公约组织
League of Nations　国家联盟

2. Interpreting Formulas

［1］It is such a delight to have friends from afar.　有朋自远方来，不亦乐乎。

［2］Mr. Smith, if my memory serves, your last visit was five years ago, wasn't it?　史密斯先生，我记得您上一次到访应该是5年前了吧？

［3］I believe that your current visit will create many trade and business opportunities for us.　我相信你们此次来访肯定会为我们双方的贸易和商业发展创造不少的机会。

［4］The Canton Fair was completely moved into the Pazhou Complex, adopting a significant reform of 3 phases in 1 session.　广交会整体移师琶洲展馆举办，实行一届三期的重大改革。

［5］I would like to take this opportunity to extend my invitation to you, Mr. Mayor, to pay a visit to our beautiful city at your earliest convenience.　我想借此机会向市长阁下发出邀请，请阁下尽早到我们美丽的城市参观访问。

［6］We have reached many censuses, which I am sure serve as solid foundation for today's deliberation.　双方已达成多方面的共识，相信为今天的交谈打下了良好的基础。

［7］We should also involve the researches of our two counties to work on the mechanism for design and implementation of patented technology and products.　我们应发展

Chapter 13 Diplomatic Interpreting 政治外交口译

由双方的研究人员共同设计执行的专利技术产品的机制。

[8] As is stipulated in the eleventh five-year plan, by the year of 2010, the energy consumption per unit GDP will decrease by 20%.   根据"十一五"规划,在 2010 年中国要比 2005 年单位 GDP 能耗减少 20%。

[9] The key is to make people conscious of the fact that small details in our life will make a big deal to our environmental protection.   关键是让民众意识到,生活中的小细节对环保的贡献也是巨大的。

[10] I hope that China will not repeat the mistakes of America and strike a balance between economic development and environmental protection.   我希望中国不要重蹈美国的覆辙,在经济发展和环境保护上取得平衡。

[11] Earlier this year, during Premier Wen Jiabao's Journey of Confidence to Europe, Switzerland was the first country he visited.   在今年年初的时候,温家宝总理出访欧洲的"信心之旅",第一个国家就选择了瑞士。

[12] Statistics show that in the year of 2007, the Sino-Swiss trade volume registered a hiking increase and Switzerland experienced trade surplus to China.   根据有关资料统计,在 2007 年,中瑞两国之间的贸易额增长幅度非常大,而且瑞士在对华贸易中处于顺差地位。

[13] Switzerland is known as a permanent neutral country.   瑞士是永久的中立国。

[14] Because of the complementarities of our economies, because of our mutual respects among our leaders, we can closer our ties and I will do my best to establish a closer partnership.   因为我们两国的经济有很强的互补性,而且两国领导人都相互尊重,我们可以发展更紧密的关系,而我也会尽我所能,使两国的关系朝着更密切的合作方向发展。

Ⅲ. Liaison Interpreting Practice

Dialogue 1

Scenario: *An American Municipal Delegation, Led by Mr. Smith* (*E*), *Is Paying an Official Visit to Guangzhou and Received by the Mayor of Guangzhou* (*C*).

C: 史密斯先生,欢迎您的到访!首先请允许我代表广州市政府再次向您和代表团的来访表示热烈的欢迎。你们一路**还顺利吧**?[1]

E: Well, it took us 14 hours to fly from U.S. to China and 1 hour drive to get here. We are a bit tired after the long journey, but your enthusiasm has cheered us up and make us feel home.

C：好啊！中国是礼仪之邦，中国人一向都非常好客。古语有云："**有朋自远方来，不亦乐乎。**"你们从太平洋的彼岸而来，就是我们的贵客，我们非常乐意招待你们。[2]

E：Thank you for your wonderful hospitality. My delegation is very grateful to you and your entire team for receiving us.

C：不客气！史密斯先生，我记得您上一次到访应该是5年前了吧？

E：Surely yes. You have a good memory! Since my last visit, I have been looking forward to my next visit to Guangzhou and **voila**! [3]

C：5年前您的来访促成了我们两市缔结友好城市的关系，我希望5年后您的再次到访能为我们两市人民取得更多的成果。

E：Thank you for your compliment. I must say that last visit was truly successful and I am expecting this one will bring more benefits for our twin cities. We are going to meet representatives from enterprises, manufacturing factories, sales agents, pharmaceutical companies, and foreign trade officials.

C：我相信你们此次来访肯定会为我们双方的贸易和商业发展创造不少的机会。说起这个，你们有没有打算顺道去广交会参观一下呢？

E：I have been to the Canton Fair during my last visit, and this time, some of our delegation members will squeeze some time from the schedule to look around in the Canton Fair exhibition complex. I heard that the venue of Canton Fair was moved to another place, wasn't it?

C：是的，第104届广交会以"新展馆、新展期、新机遇"为标志，整体移师琶洲展馆举办，实行一届三期的重大改革。这一改革取得了很好的效果，以第105届中国进出口商品交易会为例，共有21 709家参展商参展出口展区，395家参展进口展区，出口累计成交额达262.3亿美元。

E：I am impressed by what the Canton Fair has achieved and I have no doubt that my delegation members will find the visit to the Canton Fair rewarding.

C：自从我们建立友好城市以来，我们两市之间的贸易额就以每年5.7%的速度增长。此次你们会见工商界的人士，并参观广交会，我相信我们两个城市的贸易额会**更上一层楼**。[4]

Chapter 13　Diplomatic Interpreting 政治外交口译

E: I cannot agree with you more.

C: 最后，我祝愿我们两市的关系更为密切，两市人民的生活更美好！
E: Thank you very much, Mr. Mayor. I would like to take this opportunity to extend my invitation to you, Mr. Mayor, to pay a visit to our beautiful city at your earliest convenience so that we can return your warm hospitalities we have received today. [5]

C: 谢谢你的邀请！我一定会**尽早**到你们美丽的家乡参观的！[5]
E: Great! See you!

Dialogue 2

Scenario: *A Director of the Provincial Environmental Protection Bureau, Mr. Wang (W) Is Receiving a Representative, Mr. Louis Sean (L), from Environmental Protection Administration.*

W: 欢迎路易斯阁下来我局访问。我局和贵部在过去数年间一直讨论环境保护、能源和气候变化问题，双方达成多方面的共识，相信为今天的交谈打下了良好的基础。

L: I am delighted to see that we have achieved a lot in the endeavours of environmental protection. As a matter of fact, we have more room to engage active cooperation in this noble **enterprise**. [1]

W: 谢谢您对我们工作的肯定。您提到我们有更多空间可以合作，我想听一下您的高见，能否详细说一下？

L: All right. Firstly, we must continue our strategic economic dialogue pertaining to the issues of clean energy and climate change. We may deliberate on the opportunities of developing clean energies with the joint efforts of our two countries. We should also involve the researches of our two counties to work on the mechanism for design and implementation of patented technology and products.

W: 我们十分同意。我们双方应该坚持在战略经济对话合作框架下达成的有关环保、能源、气候变化领域的十年合作框架。

L: Sure. Building on the US-China Ten-Year Energy and Environment Cooperation Framework, we should expand our bilateral cooperation. I am very happy to see that China has made every effort to contribute to the **Copenhagen Climate Summit** and I am convinced that Chinese economy and policies will make greater contribution to the emission reduction. [2]

W: 确实，我们双方应更紧密地合作。从1980年到2000年20年间，我国的能源效率增加了一倍。根据"十一五"规划，在2010年中国要比2005年单位GDP能耗减少20%，我国政府在应对气候变暖和环保等议题上的决心是坚决的。

L: The efforts made by the Chinese government are applaudable. Clearly, it shows what an importance the Chinese national leaders attach to the environmental issue. I believe that the endeavour of sustainable development in China will be promising.

W: 据报道，到2020年，发达国家要在1990年基础上将温室气体排放量削减25%到40%。作为环保机构的官员之一，您觉得完成这个目标有压力吗？

L: I think the goal is achievable, technically speaking. The agency where I am serving is dedicated to setting up modern power grid, green architecture and design, and renovation of office buildings across all governments to make them more energy efficient. We also ask the countrymen to take initiative to adopt the Three R Principles and to use **renewable energy** and become more minded about energy efficient. [3]

W: 在教育民众方面，我相信你们取得了比较好的成果，您觉得我处在这方面有什么是可以借鉴的呢？

L: We ask people to think about the environmental impacts as much as possible in their daily life. For example, people use compact fluorescent lamps, instead of incandescent lamps. We also launch education campaign, to disseminate the knowledge of classification of waste. The key is to make people conscious of the fact that small details in our life will make a big deal to our environmental protection.

Chapter 13　Diplomatic Interpreting 政治外交口译

W：是的。我国也有类似的做法，例如自去年6月1日起，在所有超市、商场、集贸市场等商品零售场所实行**塑料袋有偿使用制度**，一律不得免费提供塑料购物袋。［4］这样有效控制了"白色污染"和环境恶化。

L：I have heard of this policy before and feel that it is a remarkable policy made by the Chinese government. We should all start from our daily life and make our Chinese life greener and more sustainable. I really hope that governments of all levels across China will always implement the policy and never repeat the American mistakes.

W：你所说的重蹈美国的覆辙是指什么呢？

L：Well, in the American history, there was once a time when the oil price was rocketing and people started to encourage the use of better **gas mileage** cars. ［5］But when the oil price went down, people began to forget the importance of energy efficiency and use the **inefficient cars**. I hope that China will not repeat the mistakes of America and strike a balance between economic development and environmental protection.

W：我完全同意，非常高兴看到您对我们的工作如此关注。最后，衷心感谢您来访！

Dialogue 3

Scenario：*An Anchor (A) from a Chinese TV Station Is Interviewing the Newly Appointed Swiss Ambassador (E) to China.*

A：首先我们对大使先生的到来表示特别的欢迎，也谢谢您接受我们的采访。我们的第一个问题是这样的：您去年来中国出任瑞士**驻华大使**，请问大使先生从上任到现在，最大的感受是什么？［1］

E：Well, what strikes me most is the optimism and confidence exhibited by the Chinese people for their future economy. The global community is confronted by the economic crisis, including people in Europe, America and Asia, but what I see here in China is more about their determination for a stronger economy, despite the financial crisis.

联络口译

A：您之前在泰国、缅甸、老挝、柬埔寨等国家担任过瑞士驻当地的大使。这次您到中国来担任大使，从您个人的外交生涯来说，对您来说会不会是一次新的挑战？

E：I would say that my previous experience is a very good introduction to my current responsibilities in China. But I would also like to say that Southeast Asia is not like China. Chinese people are more direct in expressing themselves and more pragmatic in dealing with people to people relationship.

A：在今年年初的时候，温家宝总理出访欧洲的"**信心之旅**"，第一个国家就选择了瑞士，您对此是如何评价的？[2]

E：We are very delighted that Premier Wen visited Switzerland as the first stop in his trip to Europe. As you know, European Union is not the whole Europe and there are countries which are not included in the EU. Switzerland is one of the non-EU countries and was also among the very first to recognise the People's Republic of China. So it is fitting that Premier Wen chose Switzerland as the first stop of his trip.

A：在我们两国的关系中，贸易关系是十分重要的。根据有关资料统计，在2007年的时候，中瑞两国之间的贸易额增长幅度非常大，而且瑞士在对华贸易中是处于一个**顺差**的地位，您能解释一下瑞士为什么会处于顺差的地位吗？[3]

E：As you said, we registered a trade surplus with China over the past few years. China now is the Switzerland's largest trading partner in Asia. Why did we have the trade surplus with China? Because the exported products of our two countries are of high complementarities and Switzerland not only exports traditional luxury products, like watches, to China, but also exports hi-tech machinery to China.

A：说到金融贸易，我们看到前段时间中国证监会批准了中国一所证券公司同瑞士信贷共同出资设立有限责任公司，而这次的合作被大家称为是"顺畅的联姻"。您是如何看待这次联姻的呢？

E：As I see it, this joint venture will provide to the Chinese market and mainland Chinese investors more investment possibilities. When Chinese businessmen make a decision in this joint venture, they will benefit from the experience of their foreign partners. I am glad to see this gradual convergence in the financial cooperation. I think we are in the **two-way street** not in **the one-way** street and we will both end up win-win. [4]

Chapter 13 Diplomatic Interpreting 政治外交口译

A：瑞士是永久的中立国，能不能给大家解释一下，"中立国"的含义是什么？

E：Neutrality of Switzerland has been shaped by history and geography. We are surrounded by big neighbours and we decided in 16th or 17th century that we would not take part in wars. Neutral means that you refuse to take part in any alliance or military pact.

A：但是在国际外交复杂的形势之下，你们如何在国际事务中保持中立呢？

E：To be neutral does not mean that you abstain from giving your opinion. Being neutral only means that you do not enter any military alliance or pact, which might basically prevent you from staying away from a conflict, should a conflict occur. For instance, we will never enter, for instance, **NATO**, which is the North Atlantic Treaty Organization, with a view to making Switzerland safer or more defending. [5]

A：我们知道日内瓦受到了众多国际组织的青睐，许多国际组织的总部就设在日内瓦，不知道是不是与瑞士的中立有关？

E：Yes, it does. Originally, it started from the League of Nations, which is the predecessor of the United Nations organization. The status of neutrality, coupled with other Swiss features, like discretion, respect for the international organizations, all that explains why increasingly international organizations establish their headquarters in Geneva.

A：今天非常感谢大使先生与我们聊了有关中国和瑞士之间的问题。在节目的最后，您想对我们的电视机前面的观众说点什么吗？

E：To our Chinese friends, I would like to say that although Switzerland is a small country with a small population, it is an important partner for China. We share common concerns for many problems and issues. Because of the complementarities of our economies, because of our mutual respects among our leaders, we can closer our ties and I will do my best to establish a closer partnership.

A：今天非常感谢大使先生，我们在这里衷心祝愿您在中国生活愉快！

Ⅳ. Notes for Interpreting

Dialogue 1

1. 本句是中文常见的问候语，但不能直译为英文。译员应该根据场合译为相应的英文问候语：Did you enjoy your flight? 如果是坐火车或汽车的话，就是 Did you enjoy your ride?

2. "有朋自远方来，不亦乐乎"，这是接待客人时经常会碰到的一句古语。本句的译文为 "It is such a delight to have friends coming from afar" 或者 "It is always a pleasure to greet friends from afar"。对于经常引用的熟语和古语，译员平时要注意积累。

3. voila 其实是法语词，但这个词已经在英语中广为应用，表示"那就是，瞧"（表示事情成功或满意之感叹词用语）。在这句话中，意思是"今天终于成行了"。另一个法语表达在英文里面也是很常见的 "C'est la vie"，意思是 This is life（生活或人生就是这样的）。英语是吸收外来词比较多的语言，因此译员也要注意积累一些常见的外来词。

4. "更上一层楼"是中文很地道的表达方式，译员不要太在意把"一层楼"的表面意思译出，只需译成"even better / greater"即可达意。当然，如果发言人引用了诗句的原文"欲穷千里目，更上一层楼"，译者就必须把这一诗句的意向传递出来"Enjoy a grander sight; by climbing to a greater height"。

5. at your earliest convenience 是比较客气的说法，中文只需要说"尽早"即可。

Dialogue 2

1. enterprise 在这里不是"企业"的意思，而是 undertaking, cause 的意思，即"事业"。译者要注意一词多义的现象，并根据词语的语境选择恰当的词义。

2. Copenhagen Climate Summit，哥本哈根气候峰会是全球气候问题的重要会议，其官方的全称是 15th United Nations Climate Change Conference（COP15）。近年来对气候问题比较重要的会议和文件包括：Kyoto Protocol《京都议定书》，United Nations Framework Convention on Climate Change《联合国气候变化框架公约》，Davos Forum（达沃斯论坛），等等。

3. renewable energy 为"可再生能源"，"不可再生能源"是 non-renewable energy。在环保问题上还有一个 3 R 原则（reduce, reuse, recycle），即"减少使用、重复使用、循环使用"，译文为了反映原文的"三"的意象，可以考虑译为"三用"原则。当然，译者也可以译为"3 R 原则，三个 R 是指三个以 R 为字母开头的单词，分别是 reduce, reuse, recycle, 意思是减少使用、重

Chapter 13　Diplomatic Interpreting 政治外交口译

复使用、循环少用。"

4. "塑料袋有偿使用制度"在口译的时候如果一下子找不到比较好的对译词，译者应该懂得变通，用"释义"（paraphrase）的方法来翻译：people have to pay for a plastic bag if they wish to use it。

5. gas mileage 原意是指"一加仑汽油所行驶的里程"，因此，better/higher gas mileage cars 是指节油汽车。相反，大耗油量汽车则是 lower gas mileage cars 或者是 inefficient cars。

Dialogue 3

1. A 国驻 B 国大使，可以译为 A's Ambassador to B。注意介词多用"to"。例如本句中的瑞士驻中国大使，英文即是 Swiss Ambassador to China。此外，"大使馆"是 embassy，"总领事馆"是 consulate general，而"总领事"则是 consul general.

2. 信心之旅 journey of confidence；友好合作之旅 journey of friendship and cooperation；破冰之旅 ice-breaking trip；融冰之旅 ice-melting trip；暖春之旅 warm-spring trip。

3. A 国对 B 国贸易顺差或逆差，可以译为 A's trade surplus/deficit to B。因此，瑞士对华顺差可以为 Swiss trade surplus to China。

4. two-way street 原意是双行道，喻指：相互帮助和关心的关系。相反，one-way street 原意是单行道，喻指：仅有单方面做出努力。

5. NATO 即：North Atlantic Treaty Organization，中文全称是北大西洋公约组织，简称北约。曾经与北约相抗衡的是 Warsaw Treaty Organization（华沙条约组织），但该组织在 1991 年宣布解散。

Chapter 14　Medical Service Interpreting
医疗服务口译
口译主题：中医中药

Ⅰ. Liaison Interpreting Tips

Nigel Wiseman once commented that "Chinese medicine is difficult to translate, and there are few people able, and even fewer people willing, to do it"①. Following his remarks, it is reasonable to assume that Chinese medicine is more difficult to interpret than to translate. Interpreting in the TCM specialty is not at all easy and the reasons are three folds.

Firstly, TCM theories and thoughts are heavily based on traditional Chinese philosophies and beliefs. Therefore, references to ancient Chinese philosophies and thoughts are ever present in the TCM prescriptions, formula and treatments. If, unfortunately, interpreters are ignorant of these ideas, they will be confronting themselves with problems of understanding TCM.

Secondly, many of the TCM expressions are culturally and linguistically unique and often correspond with no ready-made English equivalent. Interpreters and translators have to transliterate the Chinese expression and juxtapose the English explanation along. This is usually the last resort that interpreters are forced to and reluctant to adopt.

Thirdly, as TCM has a long history and has been introduced abroad for long, different English versions of TCM terms and jargons are ubiquitous in the reference books, web

---

① cf "On the qualifications of TCM translators" by Niu Chuanyue in *Journal of Chinese Integrative Medicine*, July 2004, Vol. 2, No. 4.

Chapter 14　Medical Service Interpreting 医疗服务口译

pages, brochures, and other materials alike. This will put interprets into a disadvantaged situation, where he or she is compelled to spend time not only on understanding the Chinese expressions, but also discerning the "ideal" English equivalent from a range of existing versions.

Discouraging as the interpreting task for TCM may sound, interpreters are not in the total darkness of the abyss, but in at the foot of a formidable mountain, which will be surmounted with careful preparation and sophisticated skills. As to careful preparation, interpreters must know about the task as all-encompassing as possible. TCM is composed of a series of terms and jargons, but it is not impossible to locate those commonly and frequently used terms in the Internet or books. For example, interpreters may access *WHO International Standard Terminologies on Traditional Medicine in the Western Pacific Region*①, where bilingual terms of TCM can be found. With regards to sophisticated skills, interpreters must be flexible and able to improvise during the task. Interpreters should not feel desperate to find a matching expression in the target language, because listeners understand that TCM is of utmost specialty and not every term has its linguistic counterpart. If the term is not readily available in the existing glossary, interpreters may paraphrase it or even transliterate it as the last resort.

Ⅱ. Task-based Preparation

1. Useful Expressions

Traditional Chinese Medicine (TCM)　中医
acupuncture　针(灸)
高血压　high blood pressure
穴位　(acupuncture) points
热症　heat syndrome
excessive internal heat　上火

阴阳失调　imbalance between Yin and Yang
拔火罐　cupping

---

①　The pdf version of this file can be accessed at http://www.wpro.who.int/publications/PUB 9789290612487.htm

刮痧　scraping
艾　moxa

respiratory ailments　呼吸道疾病
PMS　经前综合征
gynecological disorders　妇科疾病
gastrointestinal disorders　消化系统疾病
National Institute of Health　美国国立卫生研究院
Endorphins　内啡肽

2. Interpreting Formulas

［1］Acupuncture is famous for its special effects for diseases like high blood pressure, tension, and injuries in sports.　针灸因其独特的医治功能而闻名遐迩。患有高血压、精神紧张或者体育活动受伤的病者都可以接受针灸疗法，效果显著。

［2］"Excessive internal heat" is believed as a heat syndrome by TCM.　上火是我们中医认为的一种热证。

［3］There are several causes leading to the excessive internal heat: heart fire, liver fire, stomach fire, and lung fire.　上火分为好几种，有心火、肝火、胃火、还有肺火。

［4］It is the belief of TCM that the cause of diseases is the imbalance between Yin and Yang and to cure diseases is to restore the balance between them.　根据中医理论，疾病的发生是阴阳失调所致，而疾病的治疗就是取得阴阳之间的平衡。

［5］Generally speaking, when dealing with diseases, there are two common ways of TCM treatments: medicinal treatment and non-medicinal treatment.　大体说来，中医有两种治疗方式：药物治疗和非药物治疗。

［6］TCM favors a holistic approach, and views the universe and body philosophically.　中医着重全面的治疗，把宇宙与人体用哲学的高度来把握。

［7］Consumers perceive TCM to have slower action and milder side effects and a greater focus on treating the underlying illness versus alleviating the symptoms.　消费者认为中医药效比较慢，副作用比较温和，并更注重潜在疾病的治理，而不是减缓病征。

［8］For those that have developed to a critically late stage of illnesses, I still advocate they rely on Western Medicine as the short term cure but use TCM as the longer term fallback solution.　对于已到疾病晚期的病人，我还是建议他们采取西

Chapter 14 Medical Service Interpreting 医疗服务口译

医作为短期的治疗方式，而中医作为后备的长期的治疗方式。

[9] Acupuncture guides our "life force", Qi. It taps into specific points along the circuitry and balances the energy within all of our major organs. 针灸可引导生命之源——"气"，在经络的穴位上针灸，有助于平衡体内各主要器官的能量。

[10] In 2000, there were an estimated 11,000 licensed acupuncturists in the United States, with the number expected to double by 2010. 在2000年，美国估计有 11 000 名认证的针灸治疗师，其数目到 2010 年将会翻一番。

Ⅲ. Liaison Interpreting Practice

Dialogue 1

Scenario: *A University Student Is Asked to Accompany with His International Friend (F) to the Local Traditional Chinese Hospital for the Consultancy of Acupuncture. Please Act as the University Student and Function as a Liaison Interpreter for the Communication Between F and the Doctor (D) in the Hospital.*

F: I am fascinated by the **Traditional Chinese Medicine** [1]. Even when I was in U.S.A., I was told that acupuncture worked like magic for patients. So I am here today to get to know more about it.

D: 谢谢您对我国医学文化的关注和信赖。针灸因其独特的医治功能而闻名遐迩。患有高血压、精神紧张或者体育活动受伤的病者都可以接受针灸疗法，效果显著。

F: That is amazing. I have been experiencing some anxieties these days because I worry about the coming exams. Do you think acupuncture can help me relieve the stress?

D: 当然可以。针灸通过刺激穴位，可以让你体内的"**气**"取得平衡，从而达到舒缓身心的效果。[2]

F: Oh yes! I quite often hear about the word "Qi". I am very curious about that? Could you tell me more?

D: 气，在中医里是生命的本质。一个人的身体健康是受气体内流动影响的。

F: Well, I thought Qi meant air. It's good to know that it refers to the energy inside the body. And among many other things, I am a bit concerned about whether it is safe to have needles inserted into our body.

D: 这你可放心。针灸不是拿一根针在你身体上随便乱扎，而是在你的穴位上插一根针，而且针很细的，只要医生技术好，不但不会疼，反而有缓解疼痛的作用。

F: That really reassures me a lot. I would like to have a try right away, or do I have to book an appointment beforehand?

D: 现在恐怕不行，我们需要预约。要不您后天上午10点钟过来？

F: 10 a.m. the day after tomorrow? I am afraid I cannot make it, because I will be otherwise engaged. How about 3 p.m. on Friday afternoon?

D: 好的，没问题。

F: One more thing, my Chinese friend said I had **excessive internal heat** these days? What is "excessive internal heat"? [3]

D: 上火是我们中医认为的一种**热证**。[4]

F: Heatsyndrome? Do you mean fever?

D: 发烧只是症状之一，并不是**上火**本身。上火分为好几种，有心火、肝火、胃火、还有肺火，而且各有不一样的症状。[5]

F: So how can we extinguish the fire? It sounds that Chinese doctors are firefighters.

D: 一般来说，比较苦的或者水分多的食物都是凉性的，可以下火。

F: I have learned a lot today. See you on Friday with my first acupuncture appointment.

D: 好的，咱们到时候见。

Dialogue 2

Scenario: Your International Friend (F) Feels Better after the Treatment of Acupuncture, So He Is Much Interested in the Traditional Chinese Medicine As a Whole. He Asks You to Accompany Him to the TCM Clinic and Help Him Know More about the TCM.

Chapter 14　Medical Service Interpreting 医疗服务口译

D：早上好。针灸以后，好多了吧？
F：Much better, thank you! I do not feel stressed any more. The acupuncture is really effective.

D：我今天有什么可以帮上忙吗？
F：Yes. I come here today to know more the Traditional Chinese Medicine, or TCM. As I am fascinated by the effect of acupuncture, I begin to be obsessed with the ancient old Chinese treatments and medicines. Can you tell me something about that?
D：不错。中医有五千年的历史，它对疾病的**发生**、发展和治疗都有着完整的理论体系，针灸只不过是治疗的一种常见的方法。[1]

F：Except for this, I feel so ignorant about TCM. Would you please tell me more about it?
D：没问题。根据中医理论，疾病的发生是**阴阳**失调所致，而疾病的治疗就是取得阴阳之间的平衡。[2]

F：Well, last time we talked about Qi, which means energy, if my memory does not fail me. So what are Yin and Yang anyway?
D：对的，气即能量。阴和阳则是中国古代哲学的两个概念并代表一切事物的两个对立面。中医运用阴阳理论来解释人体的生理和病理现象。同时，阴阳也是诊断和治疗疾病的法则。

F：Then how do TCM doctors apply such theory to the treatments of patients?
D：大体说来，中医有两种治疗方式：**药物治疗**和**非药物治疗**。[3]

F：What kinds of medicinal materials do you often use for medicinal treatment? And what is non-medicinal treatment?
D：药物治疗，**中医常用**草药、矿物质、动物药等。非药物治疗包括针灸、按摩、拔火罐、刮痧等。[4]

F：I know a little about acupuncture and massage, then how about cupping?
D：拔火罐就是把一个真空的杯子吸在皮肤上引起局部充血的一种治疗方法。通常，医生把一个点燃的酒精棉球放在杯子里一会儿，以排出里面的空气使它成为一个真空杯，接着快速地把空杯子放在选定的身体表面上。

111

F: I think I have heard of **moxibustion**. [5] Is it similar with cupping or acupuncture?

D: 灸法是用燃烧的物料——通常是艾——然后直接接触皮肤表面，其热力作用于人体的穴位或特定部位。这样调节经络和内脏循环达到治愈疾病的效果。

F: Thank you very much! I've got a better understanding of TCM now.

Dialogue 3

Scenario: *A TV Anchor (A) Is Interviewing a Professor of TCM from an American University (P), Who Is Going to Talk about the Difference Between TCM and WM (Western Medicine) and the Popularity of TCM Inside and Outside China.*

A: 中医与西医之争在国内已有多时。那么，我想请教授向我们简要介绍一下西医的特点是什么？与中医有什么区别？

P: Western Medicine is known by the scientific method and emphasizes measurable biochemical processes. It also views all medical phenomena as cause-effect sequences and relies on drugs, radiation and surgery to alleviate symptoms and cure disease. On the other hand, TCM favors a holistic approach, and views the universe and body philosophically. For example, **the correct balance between Yin and Yang makes up the vital energy, "Qi", an essential life-sustaining substance of which all things are made.** [1]

A: 那么在消费者眼中，他们是怎样看待中医和西医之间的区别呢？

P: Consumers perceive TCM to have slower action and milder side effects and a greater focus on treating the underlying illness versus alleviating the symptoms. Likewise, when consumers were uncertain about their condition and not in any particular hurry for a resolution, they preferred traditional remedies. To consumers, Western Medicine treats symptoms but do not get to the root of the problem.

A: 但是消费者会不会因为中医的疗效见效慢而对中医**不太信任**？[2]

P: **Rome is not built in a day**, and neither should we expect our health problems to be fully cured by a TCM practitioner within a short period of time. [3] For those that have developed to a critically late stage of illnesses, I still advocate they rely on Western Medicine as the short term cure but use TCM as the longer term fallback solution.

Chapter 14 Medical Service Interpreting 医疗服务口译

A: 许多人说中医没有科学根据，那些药方或治疗方法都是瞎蒙的，您同意吗？

P: I am afraid I cannot support this viewpoint. Actually, the soundness of TCM is recognized to a larger and lesser extent in the international community. For example, the World Health Organization recognizes acupuncture as an effective medical treatment and has issued a list of 41 diseases amenable to acupuncture treatment. These include respiratory ailments, pain and chronic pain conditions, PMS and other gynecological disorders, gastrointestinal disorders and many other health problems.

A: 除了世界卫生组织以外，还有没有其他机构的认可呢？

P: A few years ago, the National Institute of Health published findings, which gave credits to the benefits of acupuncture. The report also classifies the clear relief and probable relief of diseases. For example, clear relief: nausea after surgery, nausea during pregnancy; pain after dental surgery. Probable relief: headaches; asthma; stroke rehabilitation, etc.

A: 那对于针灸的疗效有没有什么科学的解释呢？因为我们都很关心中医的科学根据。

P: Actually, there are some scientific proofs for acupuncture. It strengthens the immune system by increasing T-cell counts. This may be why it works on allergies and chronic syndromes. It releases pain-killing endorphins which also play a big role in the functioning of the hormonal system. Above all, acupuncture guides our "life force", Qi. It taps into specific points along the circuitry and balances the energy within all of our major organs.

A: 中医在中国十分普遍，**不知道**在美国是不是也比较受欢迎呢？教授能否为我们介绍一下中医在美国的情况？［4］

P: TCM is in fact quite popular in U.S. For example, the U.S. government has funded more than $1 million in research for the study of acupuncture's effectiveness in the treatment of addictions. Programs in **New York**, **Miami**, and **Minneapolis**, have been funded to research the treatment of drug addiction and alcoholism with acupuncture. ［5］ In 2000, there were an estimated 11,000 licensed acupuncturists in the United States, with the number expected to double by 2010.

Ⅳ. Notes for Interpreting

Dialogue 1

1. Traditional Chinese Medicine，即"中医"，相对地，"西医"是 Western Medicine。
2. "气"是中医里面很重要的一个概念，也是富有文化信息的词（culturally loaded word）。在口译的时候，译者一般可以采取"直接引用拼音 + 注释"的方式译出来。如 Qi, the energy in the body。
3. excessive internal heat 是"上火"的意思，清热则是 clearing heat。另外，"虚"一般译为 deficiency，"实"一般译为 excess。如"气虚"则是 qi deficiency。
4. 中医里面的"证"一般译为 syndrome，而"症"一般译为 symptom。
5. 在这里"火"一般译为 fire，而"热"一般译为 heat，但"上火"习惯用的是 heat，这一点要注意。另外，五行学说（five phase theory）里面的金、木、水、火、土对应的英文分别是 metal, wood, water, fire and earth。

Dialogue 2

1. "发生"在这里不宜译为 happening, occurrence。"发生"其实是指"发生的原因"，因此译为 cause 比较合适。
2. "阴阳"在英语里用的是汉语拼音。对于一些文化词，英文已经接受了用拼音的方式表达，译者就不必再用"引用拼音 + 释义"的方式，直接用拼音就可以了。例如：fengshui（风水），chop suey（杂碎），mahjong（麻将），taichi（太极）。
3. 在这里"药物治疗"和"非药物治疗"最好避免使用 drug 这一字眼，因为 drug 除了有"药"的意思外，还有"毒品"的意思，因此用 medicinal 这个词比较合适。
4. "中医常用……"这句话最好避免使用"TCM uses..."的句子来翻译，因为后面所列举均是中药的来源或原材料，因此用 traditional Chinese medicines are made from... 会比较准确。
5. moxibustion，这个词是一个音意合成词，由 moxa（日语里面"艾"的读音）加上意思 bustion（燃烧）结合而成。该词在西方国家使用已久。另外，须提出的是中文里面的"针灸"其实是 acupuncture and moxibustion，但通常普通人更多的是把"针灸"联想成"针法"，因此往往会省略后面的 moxibustion。

Chapter 14　Medical Service Interpreting 医疗服务口译

Dialogue 3

1. 由于这里是哲学意味比较浓的句子，所以译者译的时候也要注意句子要简洁，词语运用要比较典雅。如果直译为："阴阳的正确平衡构成气，气是所有事物维系生命的重要物质"，这不免让听众觉得中医哲学思想佶屈聱牙，因此应译为："阴阳均衡有助养气，气乃是万物生命之本"。

2. 如果一定要把"不太信任"的字面意思译出，那么译者只好译为 have little confidence/trust in，从而使句子结构变成 consumers have little confidence/trust in TCM, because of... 其实，可以反过来翻译，不太信任是"怀疑"的意思，那么可用 doubtful of 来翻译。

3. Room was not built in a day，意思是"罗马不是一天建起来的"，意指不是一蹴而就的。但如果用于本对话的语境，我们不妨译为"冰冻三尺，非一日之寒"，这样既符合疾病发生的情况，又符合中文的表达。

4. 这里的"不知道"重点不是要向听众表达自己"不知道"，而是"想知道"，英文有一个词是 wonder. 所以本句可以译为 I am wondering...，或者译者可以直接提出问题。

5. 这里提到三个地名，前面两个对于中国人来说较为常见，后面的一个则稍微陌生一些。译者如果在口译中不知道其中文名称，则只需要把英文的发音记住，然后翻译的时候直接读出该地名即可。

Chapter 15 Legal Service Interpreting
法律服务口译
口译主题：法律事务

Ⅰ. Liaison Interpreting Tips

Legal interpreting here falls into another specialized domain of interpreting. Court interpreting, as a typical form of legal interpreting, is commonly used in the trials which involve foreigners or people speaking any language other than the dominant one in the country.

When doing the legal interpretation, one must be aware of the following points:
1. Words that are commonly used in daily context carry other meanings in the legal context.
2. Latin words or phrases are not uncommon in legal language.
3. Legal jargons are ubiquitous.
4. Formal words or words in frozen style are frequently used.
5. Doublets and triplets are used to express the same meaning.
6. Redundancy and repetition in expressing the same meaning are common tactics to avoid ambiguities.
7. Legal interpretations usually pertain to long sentences.

This chapter, however, does not deal with Court Interpreting per se, but rather liaison interpreting in the legal context. The latter may not be as challenging as court interpreting, but not less demanding in terms of achieving accuracy and adequacy in translating meanings. In addition to all these, interpreters must keep the principle of impartiality in mind, because legal interpreting requires absolute equality for all parties concerned. To this end, interpreters are advised to get themselves fully prepared for the task by browsing the laws in the specific filed (e.g. common law, criminal law, civil

Chapter 15　Legal Service Interpreting 法律服务口译

law, etc.). A highly recommendable website for the preparatory purpose is http://www.lawyee.net, in which you have access to many bilingual versions of laws in China.

In legal interpreting, it is common that speakers will initiate the sentence as "Ask him if..." or "Tell him that...". In one word, parties will address interpreters directly instead of each other. Therefore, third-person pronoun is frequently used. In liaison interpreting, this is not unacceptable, so interpreters may delete the third-person address and simply interpret the content of the sentences. A quite note, though, is that third-person address usually implies distance and non-involvement, while second-person address often indicates intimacy and involvement. Interpreters must be able to understand the purpose of the speakers and adjust the address accordingly. For example, if the speakers persist on using "Tell him that...", interpreters may adopt the interpreting as "他说...", instead of "告诉他...".

Ⅱ. Task-based Preparation

1. Useful Expressions

就业证　employment license
就业许可证　employment permit
国家机关　government organs and institutions
工作准证　work permit
文化部　Ministry of Culture
意向书　letter of intention
资格证明　credentials
公安机关　public security organs
居留证　residence certificate
居留资格被取消　residence status is revoked

房产　real estate properties
商品房销售许可证　Commodity Housing Sale License
商品房预售许可证　Commodity Housing Pre-sale License
住房管理局　housing administrative bureau
合同税　contract tax

印花税　stamp tax

Sino-foreign equity joint ventures　中外合资经营企业
中外合资经营企业法　the Law on Sino-foreign Joint Ventures
可行性研究报告　feasibility study report
具有同等效力　shall have equal validity
tangible and non-tangible assets　有形和无形资产
工会　trade union
中华全国总工会　All China Federation of Trade Unions

2. Interpreting Formulas

［1］One must have a valid passport or other international travel document in lieu of the passport.　持有者须持有有效护照或能代替护照的其他国际旅行证件。

［2］In a certain situation foreigners may be exempted from the Employment License and Employment Permit.　在某些情况下，外籍劳工可免申领就业证和就业许可证。

［3］Foreign workers with special skills who work in offshore petroleum operations without the need to go ashore for employment and hold "Work Permit for Foreign Personnel Engaged in the Offshore Petroleum Operations in the People's Republic of China" can be exempted.　持有《外国人在中华人民共和国从事海上石油作业工作准证》从事海上石油作业、不需登陆、有特殊技能的外籍劳务人员可免申领。

［4］The employer and its foreign employee should, in accordance with law, conclude a labour contract, the term of which shall not exceed five years.　用人单位与被聘用的外国人应依法订立劳动合同。劳动合同的期限最长不得超过五年。

［5］For foreigner whose residence status is revoked by public security organs due to his violation of Chinese law, his labour contract should be terminated by his employer and his Employment Permit be withdrawn by the labour administrative authorities.　因违反中国法律被中国公安机关取消居留资格的外国人，用人单位应解除劳动合同，劳动部门应吊销就业证。

［6］Foreigners who intend to buy a house in Beijing need a certificate issued by the Beijing Municipal Public Security Bureau to prove that they have stayed in China for at least one year for reasons of work or study.　欲在北京买房的外国人需要出示由北京市公安局开具的证明，以证明其在中国工作或学习至少一年。

Chapter 15　Legal Service Interpreting 法律服务口译

［7］ There are taxes and fees that should be paid in relation to transactions. For example, a buyer of a house should pay the contract tax and stamp tax, as well as the registration fees for the property of the house and its underlying land use right. 置业者须缴付与交易有关的税费，例如，合同税、印花税，还有房产登记费和土地使用权费。

［8］ Sino-foreign equity joint ventures established within China's territory in accordance with the Law on Sino-foreign Joint Ventures are Chinese legal persons and are subject to the jurisdiction and protection of the Chinese law. 依照《中外合资经营企业法》批准在中国境内设立的中外合资经营企业是中国的法人，受中国法律的管辖和保护。

［9］ obvious inequity in the agreements, contracts and articles of association signed impairing the rights and interests of one party　签订的协议、合同、章程显属不公平，损害合营一方权益的

［10］ The value shall be assessed through consultation by the parties to the joint venture on the basis of fairness and reasonableness, or shall be assessed by a third party agreed upon by parties to the joint venture. 其作价由合营各方按照公平合理的原则协商确定，或者聘请合营各方同意的第三者评定。

Ⅲ. Liaison Interpreting Practice

Dialogue 1

Scenario: *A Foreigner (F) Is Trying to Consult from a Chinese Embassy Staff (L) about the Requirements and Submittals for Working in China.*

F: Hi, I was approached by a Chinese local company and I am interested in working in China. So I come to ask for a few pieces of information. First, what kind of conditions must **one** meet if **one** is planning to get employed in China?［1］

L: 外国劳工在中国工作**需**满足以下条件：［2］1. 年满18周岁，身体健康；2. 具有从事其工作所必需的专业技能和相应的工作经历；3. 无犯罪记录；4. 有确定的聘用单位；5. 持有有效护照或能**代替**护照的其他国际旅行证件。［3］

F: I was told that in a certain situation foreigners may be exempted from the Employment License and Employment Permit. Is it true?

L：由我政府直接出资聘请的外籍专业技术和管理人员，或由国家机关和事业单位出资聘请，具有本国或国际权威技术管理部门或行业协会确认的高级技术职称或特殊技能资格证书的外籍专业技术和管理人员，并持有外国专家局签发的《外国专家证》的外国人可免申领就业证和就业许可证。[4]

F：Is there any other situation where one may enjoy this special treatment?

L：持有《外国人在中华人民共和国从事海上石油作业工作准证》从事海上石油作业、不需登陆、有特殊技能的外籍劳务人员或文化部批准持《临时营业演出许可证》进行营业性文艺演出的外国人也可以免申领。

F：If I am to apply for the Employment License or Employment Permit, what kinds of documents must be submitted for application?

L：您需要提交：1. 拟聘用的外国人履历证明；2. 聘用意向书；3. 拟聘用外国人原因的报告；4. 拟聘用的外国人从事该项工作的资格证明；5. 拟聘用的外国人健康状况证明；6. 法律、法规规定的其他文件。[5]

F：How long may the employment contract last?

L：用人单位与被聘用的外国人应依法订立劳动合同。劳动合同的期限最长不得超过五年。劳动合同期限届满即行终止，但按相关规定履行审批手续后可以续订。

F：Can foreigners who have not been issued residence certificate (i.e. holders of F, L, C or G type visas) and those who are under study or interim programs in China work in China?

L：不可以。特殊情况应由用人单位按规定的审批程序申领许可证书，被聘用的外国人凭许可证书到公安机关改变身份，办理就业证、居留证后方可就业。

F：If the residence status is revoked, can one still be employed?

L：因违反中国法律被中国公安机关取消居留资格的外国人，用人单位应解除劳动合同，劳动部门应吊销就业证。

F：OK. I get the general picture of the relevant regulations and polices. Thank you for your help.

L：不客气！

Chapter 15　Legal Service Interpreting 法律服务口译

Dialogue 2

Scenario：*A Foreigner（F）Is Going to Buy a House in China，but He Is Not Sure about the Legal Procedure of the Transaction，So He Is Now Asking His Chinese Friend（C），Who Work in a Chinese Law Firm，for Help.*

F：I want to buy a house in Beijing, what kind of documents must I **produce**?［1］

C：欲在北京买房的外国人需要出示由北京市公安局开具的证明，以证明其在中国工作或学习至少一年。

F：What tips do you have for the foreigners who are planning to purchase real estate properties in China?

C：在购买房产前，外国居民房产须满足政府和法律的相关要求。须让销售方出示由当地政府有关部门开具的《**商品房销售许可证**》，若房子还没有建成，则须出示《**商品房预售许可证**》。［2］

F：Upon signing the sales contract, what should be taken care of?

C：在购买的时候，买卖双方通常签署一份商品房买卖销售合同，该合同由当地住房管理局拟定。合同订明一些常见的条款，如：面积和单价、建造和交易条件、开发商的保证书和以后的管理。此外，双方通常签署涉及交易的专门的条款的补充协议。

F：Are contracts written in Chinese? Are contracts in other foreign languages available?

C：合同通常是用中文写的，建议外国居民索取一份用自己本国语言写的合同。当然也可以从中国律师那里寻求帮助，现在中国的执业律师都可以讲外文和中文。

F：When buying the real property in China, should foreigners get registered in the Chinese government office?

C：外国居民在中国买卖房产须在房地产和土地管理的有关部门那里登记。否则，所做的交易不合法，卖方或买方须**按**中国有关法律登记**后**，其房产的权益**才**得到充分的保障。［3］

F：Shall I pay any kind of **tax** when I buy a property?

C：置业者须缴付与交易有关的税费，例如，合同税、印花税，还有房产登记费和土地使用权费。［4］

F: One last question, if I want to **rent my purchased house**, shall I notify the department concerned or I can simply **do so** without tell the authority? [5]

C: 如果你置业后想将其出租、转售或用作其他商业用途,你要先成立一家外资公司,然后取得相关的营业执照才可以。

Dialogue 3

Scenario: *A Multi-national Company Is Planning to Access the Chinese Market by Setting a Joint Venture in China. The Company (F) Is now Soliciting Consultation from a Chinese Law Firm (C).*

F: Is Sino-foreign equity joint ventures established in China entitled to legal person status?

C: 依照《中外合资经营企业法》批准在中国境内设立的中外合资经营企业是中国的法人,受中国法律的管辖和保护。

F: What kinds of joint ventured can be established in China?

C: 一般情况下,我们都支持各种合营企业在中国设立,但是申请设立合营企业有下列情况之一的,不予批准:1. **有损**中国主权的;2. **违反**中国法律的;3. **不符合**中国国民经济发展要求的;4. 造成环境污染的;5. 签订的协议、合同、章程**显属不公平**,**损害**合营一方权益的。[1]

F: We are doing logistics business and I think none of the conditions you mentioned previously exist in our endeavor to team up with our Chinese partner. So what kinds of documents must we submit for approval?

C: 申请设立合营企业,由中外合营者共同向审批机构报送下列文件:1. 设立合营企业的申请书;2. 合营各方共同编制的可行性研究报告;3. 由合营各方授权代表签署的合营企业协议、合同和章程;4. 由合营各方委派的合营企业董事长、副董事长、董事人选名单;5. 审批机构规定的其他文件。

F: Should all these materials written in Chinese? Or English versions are also deemed acceptable?

C: 前款所列文件必须用中文书写,其中第2,3,4项文件可以同时用合营各方商定的一种外文书写。两种文字书写的文件**具有同等效力**。[2]

Chapter 15　Legal Service Interpreting　法律服务口译

F: How do the parties to the joint venture share their **liability**?［3］

C: 合营企业为**有限责任公司**。合营各方对合营企业的责任以各自认缴的出资额为限。

F: How does each party to the joint venture contribute their shares? Should it be solely on cash basis or tangible and non-tangible assets are also available?

C: 合营者可以用货币出资，也可以用建筑物、厂房、机器设备或者其他物料、工业产权、专有技术、场地使用权等作价出资。以建筑物、厂房、机器设备或者其他物料、工业产权、专有技术作为出资的，其作价由合营各方按照公平合理的原则协商确定，或者聘请合营各方同意的第三者评定。［4］

F: Is the joint venture allowed to open bank accounts in and outside China to deal with the settlement and fiscal services?

C: 合营企业凭营业执照，在境内银行开立外汇账户和人民币账户，由开户银行监督收付。合营企业在国外或者港澳地区的银行开立外汇账户，应当经国家外汇管理局或者其分局批准，并向国家外汇管理局或者其分局报告收付情况和提供银行对账单。

F: Upon the establishment of the joint venture, is there any rule governing the deployment of personnel? For example, should the senior management posts be taken by the Chinese citizens only or the posts are also open for the foreign counterparts?

C: 总经理、副总经理由合营企业董事会聘请，可以由中国公民担任，也可以由外国公民担任。

F: Does the joint venture **assume** any obligation to support the trade union? Or the trade union will take care of itself?［5］

C: 合营企业应当积极支持本企业工会的工作。合营企业每月按企业职工实际工资总额的2%拨交工会经费，由本企业工会按照中华全国总工会制定的有关工会经费管理办法使用。

Ⅳ. Notes for Interpreting

Dialogue 1

1. 注意问句中使用了正式语体的 one 而没有用 you 或 I。在口译中，这个 one 可以

123

不译出来,因为中文可以接受无主句的情况。
2. 这里简要讲述 shall/must/may 的区别。这三个词语在法律文本上出现的频率较多,因此其对应译文应予以关注。shall 一般翻译为"应当","需要";must 一般翻译为"必须";may 一般翻译为"可以"。
3. in lieu of 是比较正规的用法,表示"以……来代替"。
4. 长句是法律英语的一大特点。我们可以把意思切分成以下几个部分:"由 A 我政府直接出资聘请的外籍专业技术和管理人员,或 B1 由国家机关和事业单位出资聘请,B2 具有本国或国际权威技术管理部门或行业协会确认的高级技术职称或特殊技能资格证书的外籍专业技术和管理人员,并持有 C 外国专家局签发的《外国专家证》的外国人可免申领就业证和就业许可证。"这句话指的是在 A + C 或 B1 + B2 + C 两种情况下可以免申领。
5. 这句话列举了 6 个部分的内容。如果记笔记时,记不了那么多的话,可以适当省略,然后用"等等"概而述之。但是本句中的 6 个部分都是必须的,缺一不可的。因此,译员只能逐一记下,遇到遗漏记不住的部分要请讲话人再讲一次。

Dialogue 2

1. produce 在这里的意思是 "show or provide (something) for consideration, inspection, or use",中文可译为"出示"。该义项在日常英语中较少遇见,译者需留心。
2. "商品房销售许可证"是 Commodity Housing Sale License;"商品房预售许可证"是 Commodity Housing Pre-sale License。
3. 如果按照中文的句型"……后……才"用"after...then"来翻译是可以的,但是英文有更好的词 until,因此可以处理成 the property are not sufficiently protected until it has been……
4. "税"是 tax,"费"是 fee。本句提到的"合同税、印花税"可译成"contract tax","stamp tax"。其他比较普遍的税还有:所得税(income tax),营业税(business tax),奢侈品税(luxury tax),销售税(sales tax),劳务税(service tax)。
5. rent my purchased house 意思是"购买后想出租"的意思。此外,英文的行文习惯是不喜欢重复,所以原文用了"do so"来代替"rent the house",但是汉语的行文习惯允许重复,因此英文中可以两次都翻译成"出租"。

Dialogue 3

1. 这句话中"有损"、"违反"、"不符合"、"损害"分别对应为 detriment to;violation of;nonconformity with;impairing。
2. "具有同等效力"是 both versions shall have equal validity,但是如果是"以中文版

Chapter 15　Legal Service Interpreting　法律服务口译

本为准"则是 the English version shall prevail。

3. liability 是指 the state of being responsible for something, especially by law, 尤指法律上的责任。"有限责任公司"则是 limited liability company, 简称 LLC。

4. 在本句中"建筑物、厂房、机器设备或其他物料、工业产权、专有技术"出现了两次。由于法律英语会重复一些关键的信息来避免歧义或误解，因此在口译时该部分也要悉数译出。

5. "assume"是一个比较正式的词语，比"shoulder"或"take"都要正式。因此"assume the obligation"译成"有责任……"即可。

Answers for Reference
口译练习参考答案

Chapter 2　Etiquette of Receiving Guests　接待礼仪
口译主题：外宾接待

Dialogue 1

1.1

A：Excuse me. Are you Mr. Jackson from the U.S.?

B：正是。

A：Nice to meet you, Mr. Jackson. I'm Wayne Wong from the China Tourist Agency. Welcome to Guangzhou!

B：很高兴见到您，维恩。谢谢您来接我。

A：My pleasure. I'll be your tour guide and interpreter during your stay in China.

B：好的。谢谢。

1.2

A：Hi, Mr. Jackson. Haven't seen you for ages!

B：您好，维恩。是的，我们上次在上海见面是3年前。

A：How have you been doing?

B：很好。您呢?

A：Just fine. I hope your will enjoy your stay here in Guangzhou.

B：肯定愉快。

Dialogue 2

2.1

A：Did you have a nice trip?

B: 感觉不错。

A: Oh, I'm glad to hear that. That's the best thing you can say about a flight, isn't it?

B: 当然啦。

2.2

A: Do you feel tired after the long trip?

B: 是有点累，可我更觉得有点兴奋。

A: Would you like to go to the hotel and have a rest before supper?

B: 好的。

Dialogue 3

A: Is this your first trip to China?

B: 是的，一切感觉都很新鲜。

A: China is a beautiful country. I'm sure you will have a nice trip here.

B: 希望如此。

A: What is your first impression of this city?

B: 我对这个城市的繁荣景象印象深刻。

A: Yes, great changes have taken place in our city. It's becoming more and more prosperous.

B: 我很喜欢看到这样一个多姿多彩、充满活力的城市。

A: By the way, I've made a reservation for you at White Swan Hotel.

B: 好的，谢谢。什么时候能到？我希望尽快安顿下来。

A: We will arrive at the hotel in half an hour.

B: 太好了。

Dialogue 4

A: OK, here we are. We'll check in at the front desk.

B: 您已经预定好了房间，需要我做些什么？

A: Just fill in the registration form, please.

B: 好的。我需要出示我的护照吗？

A: Yes, please. They'll have to confirm your passport number.

B: 好的，给您。

联络口译

Chapter 3　Tour Guiding　导游口译
口译主题：旅游导览

Dialogue 1

1.1

A：The Yellow Mountain is famous for its Four Wonders—fantastic pines, grotesque rocks, the sea of clouds and hot springs.

B：这里的温泉水是可饮用的吗？

A：Yes, it is. The hot spring water gushes out from the Purple Cloud Peak at 42℃ all year round. It is clear, tasteless, colorless and non-poisonous.

B：看那些云！这里的云雾真像海上的波澜，云雾中的山峰就像大海中的岛屿。

A：Yes. Look at those pines. On the left are the Lion Rock and Welcoming Pine which has stretched its boughs to welcome tourists up the mountain. On the right are the Elephant Rock and Farewell Pine which has extended its branches to say goodbye to tourists down the mountain.

B：山上这么多好看的景点和风景！真是不虚此行。

1.2

A：Known as a Paradise on Earth, Hangzhou enjoys pleasant climate and picturesque landscape. The beauty of Hangzhou is associated with the West Lake.

B：我听说西湖有"十景"，是哪十景？

A：Well. They are Spring at the Su Causeway, Autumn Moon over the Calm Lake, Viewing Fish at Flower Harbor, Listening to Orioles in the Willows, Twin Peaks Piercing to the Clouds, Three Pools Mirroring the Moon, Sunset View of Leifeng Tower, Evening Bell of the Southern Screen, Lotus in the Breeze at Crooked Courtyard, and Remaining Snow on the Broken Bridge.

B：我们今天都能去到吗？

A：No, I'm afraid we can't. But we'll try to see most of them.

Dialogue 2

2.1

A：The Great Wall is a must-see spot in Beijing, just like the pyramids in Egypt.

Answers for Reference 口译练习参考答案

B：我听说万里长城是世界奇迹之一。

A：Yes, it runs all the way across the northern half of China with a length of 6,350 km, or 12,700 Chinese li. That's why we call it Ten-Thousand-li Great Wall.

B：真让人印象深刻！

A：You know there is a popular Chinese saying about ascending the Wall. It goes, "If one fails to climb to the top of the Great Wall, he is not a true man."

B：那我们登上了长城，都是好汉了！

2.2

A：Suzhou is a city with a long history of about 2,500 years. It is world-famous especially for its landscaped gardens.

B：苏州园林有何特别？

A：There're about 150 gardens in Suzhou. Some of them are more than 1,000 years old. These gardens are not large but curious in their designs, and their designs are based on inspiration of poets and imagination of painters. They bring together the beauties of nature, architecture and painting.

B：真吸引人！今天我想专门游览苏州的园林。

A：No problem. Today we will visit the most famous ones: the Lion Grove Garden, the Humble Administrator Garden, the Lingering Garden, the Master of Nets Garden.

Dialogue 3

3.1

A：看这些画，真让人叹为观止！

B：Yes, Chinese painting has incorporated the best of many forms of art, like poetry, calligraphy and seal engraving.

A：这幅竹画画得真好！为什么中国人喜欢画松、竹、梅？

B：In Chinese culture, pines, bamboo and plum are meant to embody the qualities of people who are upright and show good moral behavior, so they become favorite subjects for Chinese painters.

A：画上有印章，起什么作用？

B：The inscriptions and seals on the paintings not only can help us understand the painter's ideas and emotions, but also add decorative beauty.

A：从美学角度来看，中国画与西方画有不少共通之处，但它也独具民族特色，对吗？

B: Yes. Chinese paintings can be divided into five categories according to the format: murals, screens, scrolls, and albums and fans.

A: 中国画的主题有哪些?

B: The subjects of Chinese paintings include figures, landscapes, buildings, and flowers.

A: 听说最有名的一位中国画大师是齐白石,对吗?

B: Yes, Qi was a skillful poet, painter, calligrapher and seal-cutter. He is an artistic giant of the 20th century.

3.2

A: 你们中国人是如何品鉴玉器的?

B: Standards used to gauge the value of jade are hardness, mellow color, smoothness and pleasant sound.

A: 玉器很珍贵吗?

B: Of course. People even believe that jade has divine and supernatural forces. Characteristics of jade are elaborate and beautiful patterns, fluent lines and complicated images.

A: 为什么人们要打制装饰玉器?

B: Well, the jade pieces in Chinese culture are made not only for the sake of art; they also have mysterious meanings and functions.

A: 有些什么意义和作用,能说说吗?

B: Yes. Primitives believed that jade could make the soul immortal and preserve corpses. In the Spring and Autumn Period, people compared human virtues to pure jade. Its hardness suggested firmness and loyalty, and its luster projected purity and beauty.

Dialogue 4

4.1

A: 这是我第一次来广州,我想游览一些城市景点。

B: There're many tourist attractions in Guangzhou. Best known are the Baiyun Mount, the Yuexiu Park, Sun Yetsen's Memorial Hall, the Chen Clan Academy and the Nanyue Mausoleum Museum.

A: 你有这些景点的资料吗?

B: Let me give you some brochures to look over.

A：我对陈家祠很感兴趣，您能给我多介绍一点吗？
B：Sure. The Chen Clan Academy is one of the biggest clan academies in Guangdong Province, as well as the representative of Lingnan architectural decoration and arts.

4.2

A：今天我想游览上海，看一些著名景点。
B：Good idea. The Yuyuan Garden, The Jade Buddha Temple and The Bund are all tourist attractions in the city.
A：噢，我有点迫不及待了，可是我只有一天时间，怎样可以一天游览所有这些景点呢？
B：In that case I suggest you call a cab, or take a sightseeing coach.

Chapter 4　Dining & Cuisine　宴请口译
口译主题：宴请饮食

Dialogue 1

A：Good evening! What can I get for you?
B：有什么餐前小食品？
A：Yes. This is our menu of appetizers. How about some pickles?
B：好的，我们来点儿。
A：Then what would you like for the main course?
B：今晚有什么特别推荐的？
A：Yes, Sir. We are featuring beef steak with baked potato.
B：好的，我要这个。
A：Would you like something for your dessert? We've got very good vanilla ice-cream.
B：不用，谢谢！
A：Anything to drink?
B：请上红酒。
A：OK. Thank you!

Dialogue 2

A：This way, please. Mr. Jackson, please take your seat.
B：谢谢！谢谢你请我吃饭。
A：It's my great pleasure. We're honored to have you from afar visit our company. I wish we can have a good beginning of our cooperation.

131

B：我想肯定可以。谢谢贵方的友好情谊和盛情款待!

A：I have ordered Chinese food for this evening. I hope you will like it.

B：很好。中国菜世界知名，能到中国品尝中国菜，我很幸运!

A：What would you like to drink, beer, wine or liquor?

B：我要啤酒吧。

A：Well, Mr. Jackson, I'd like to propose a toast to our friendship and cooperation.

B：好的。为我们的友谊和合作，干杯!

Dialogue 3

A：你们中国人如何品鉴中国菜?

B：We judge Chinese food by three key elements: "color, aroma and taste".

A：有意思! 如何评判菜肴的"色"?

B：The "color" of Chinese food, as the first of these elements, is evident in the layout and design of dishes in a Chinese banquet.

A：那么"香"呢?

B："Aroma" implies more than what one's nose can detect directly; it also includes the freshness of the raw materials used and the blending of seasonings.

A：那么"味"呢?

B："Taste" is the art of proper seasoning, though it also involves the texture of food and fine slicing techniques.

A：真是了不起! 厨师如何能做到"色、香、味"兼具?

B：These three essential elements, "color", "aroma", "taste", are achieved by the careful coordination of a series of delicate activities: selecting ingredients, mixing flavor, timing the cooking, controlling the heat and finally, laying out the food on the plate for the table.

A：能给我介绍一下中国宴席上喝酒的礼仪吗?

B：No problem. In Chinese banquet, people will usually "Gan Bei" when toasting each other. "Gan Bei" means to raise up one's glass and drink it all the way down so that the glass is "dried up to the last drop". People dry up their glasses to communicate the message to guests that they are sincere in respecting guests and joyful in friendly gathering.

A：我一定要"干杯"吗? 那我很快就会醉了。

B：You don't have to. For a foreign guest, it is quite acceptable to take a sip instead of emptying the glass when toasting with his or her Chinese host.

Answers for Reference 口译练习参考答案

Chapter 5　Exhibitions & Fairs　展会口译
口译主题：参展参会

Dialogue 1

1.1

A：世博园区的结构是如何设计的？

B：Various buildings within the Expo Site would create a series of marvelous sceneries, where visitors would be rendered into a future "global village". The Expo Site would be a five-level structure, namely "Park, Area, Zone, Group, Cluster".

A：真特别！"园、区"指什么？

B：The "Park" refers to the land scope of 5.28 square kilometers for Expo 2010. The "Area" refers to the Enclosed Area of 3.28 square kilometers. The Enclosed Area will require admission by ticket.

A："片、组、团"呢？

B：There are five functional zones within the "Park", each of which known as "Zone". The five functional zones are marked A, B, C, D and E respectively, for easy distinguishing. The "Group" represents several pavilion groups within each "Zone". Each "Group" also contains several pavilion clusters, each of which known as "Cluster".

1.2

A：能给我介绍一些世博园区的主要参观点吗？

B：Sure. First the theme pavilions. The theme for Expo 2010 covers five dimensions: "Urbanian", "City Being", "Urban Planet", "Footprint" and "Dream", which are accordingly represented by five theme pavilions. The Urbanian Pavilion, Pavilion of City Being and Pavilion of Urban Planet are located in Pudong Site, using newly-built pavilion. Pavilion of Urban Civilization and Pavilion of Future are situated in Puxi Site; they will be renovated from existing industrial building.

A：中国馆在哪个位置？

B：The China Pavilion is located at the projecting area near the main entrance of Pudong Site, within Zone B of the Enclosed Area. It comprises the Chinese National Pavilion, Chinese Provinces Pavilion, and Pavilion of Hong Kong, Macao and Taiwan.

— 133 —

A：我听不少人提到中国馆，它很特别吗？

B：Surely it is. The exterior design of China Pavilion is based on the concept of "Oriental Crown", to express the spirit and disposition of Chinese culture. Rising from the center, the Chinese National Pavilion is supported by traditional *Dougong* brackets fixed layer upon layer, concentrating Chinese elements and embodying Chinese spirit. The Chinese Provinces Pavilion extends in flat under the Chinese National Pavilion, serving as a reliable platform, to build an open, mild, compatible and rich layered city square.

A：有什么地方可以俯瞰整个园区吗？

B：The Harmony Tower is situated to the east of the Pavilion of Future. At the top of the Harmony Tower, you may enjoy a birds-eye view over the whole Expo Site.

A：你还会推荐哪些参观景点？

B：Eh, I would recommend the Theme Square, which is located to the west of the Theme Pavilion; the Expo Park, which is within Pudong Site, along the Huangpu River; the Expo Village, which is located on the northeast part of Pudong Site; the Urban Best Practices Area, which is within Zone E, Puxi Site, adjacent to the Nanpu Bridge.

A：看来有很多好玩的地方，我怎样能方便地看到各个点呢？

B：The Elevated Pedestrians' Walk may guide you to all pavilions.

1.3

A：世博会除了国家馆，还有哪些展馆？

B：There are International Organization Pavilions, Theme Pavilions, and Corporate Pavilions.

A：企业馆有多少个？

B：The Corporate Pavilions always constitute one of the highlights in world expositions. There will be about 16 Corporate Pavilions at Expo 2010.

A：听起来很让人期待！国际组织馆呢，好看吗？

B：For sure, they must be as splendid as the National Pavilions!

A：所有的展馆都是独立的吗？

B：No, There are stand-alone pavilions, joint pavilions, and rented pavilions built by the Expo Organizer.

Dialogue 2

A：这是我第一次参加广交会，你能给我做个总体介绍吗？

B：The complete name of the Canton Fair is "the China Import and Export Fair". It is held in Guangzhou twice a year in spring and autumn since 1957. Until spring of 2010, 107 Sessions have been held.

A：噢，举办得很成功！广交会怎么会这么成功呢？

B：The Fair, comprehensive in nature, has won its fame of "China's No. 1 Fair" for the longest history, the highest level, the largest scale, the most complete exhibit variety, the broadest buyer distribution, the biggest buyer attendance, the greatest business turnover, and the best credit standing in China.

A：那也就是说，这个展会参与面很广？

B：Every year thousands of foreign trade enterprises with good credibility and sound financial capability take part in the Fair, including foreign trade companies, factories, scientific research institutions, foreign invested enterprises, private enterprises.

A：我迫不及待想亲眼看看！广交会的地点在哪里？

B：It is in the China Import and Export Fair Complex, at Pazhou.

Dialogue 3

A：Good morning. Welcome to the Canton Fair!

B：谢谢！请问你们公司是做什么生意的？

A：Ours is a company specializing in exporting pure silk carpets.

B：太好了！我公司对真丝地毯很有兴趣。

A：What kind of design would you like?

B：中国式样和土耳其式样的都要。

A：And what size do you want?

B：小挂毯，长四英尺，宽3英尺。请问到12月上旬你们能生产多少？

A：That depends on how many you wish to purchase.

B：我要一万条。

A：That's a lot. I'm afraid I can't promise you 10,000 by early December, but can confirm 5 000.

B：谢谢。每条单价是多少？

A：We have a fixed wholesale price for this carpet. That's $30 each.

B：但是我们的采购量很大呀……

A：OK. We can offer you a 5% discount.

B：嗯，不错。

Chapter 6　Business Negotiations　谈判口译
口译主题：商务洽谈

Dialogue 1

A：Glad to meet you, Mr. Smith. I'm the sales representative. My family name is Wang and here is my name card. Can I help you?

B：可以，我对你们的儿童系列玩具有兴趣。

A：Right. We've got some new models here. The toys on the right are machine toys, electronic toys, electrical toys and intellectual toys, suitable for children from the age of five upwards. The toys on the left are bamboo wooden toys, plastic toys and plush toys, suitable for children under five. They are all available from stock.

B：嗯，不错。

A：They've only been on the market for a few months, but they are already very popular.

B：价格如何？

A：Here is the price list.

B：谢谢。何时能够发货？

A：We can deliver the goods within the days upon receipt of your order.

B：订购量大的话，能否给点儿优惠价？

A：Well, it depends on the size of the order. I'll have to check for specifics. Would you mind waiting for a moment? Please take a look at our brochure.

B：没问题。谢谢！

Dialogue 2

A：Now that everyone is here, let's get down to business.

B：好的。很遗憾你们的报价太高，如果按这种价格买进，我方实在难以推销。

A：Well, if you take quality into consideration, you won't think our price is too high. And the price of raw materials has gone up.

B：干吗不试试各让一步呢？

A：OK. How many do you intend to order?

B：我们想订500打。

A：If your order is bulk, we may offer a better price.

B：那我的订单增加到900打吧。

A：Great. We will offer you 10% discount.

B：好的，这价格我接受。下面我想讨论一下包装问题，我们都知道，包装直接关系到产品的销售。

A：Please state your opinions.

B：我希望新包装会使我们的顾客满意，买主总是很注意包装。我希望我们的意见能传达到厂商。

A：No problem. How do you like the goods dispatched, by railway or by sea?

B：请海运发货，铁路运输费用太高，我愿意走海运。

A：That's what we think.

B：你们什么时候能交货？我非常担心货物迟交。

A：We can effect shipment in December or early next year at the latest.

B：那很好。

Dialogue 3

A：Good morning, I've brought the draft of the contract. Please go over it.

B：好的，请坐。您想喝什么，茶还是咖啡？

A：Thank you. I'd like to have a cup of tea.

B：好的。

（B 看合同）

A：Finished?

B：看完了。关于第 8 款我有个问题，这是我们议定的条款吗？

A：OK. Let's have a look at it.

B：百分之十付现款，余额在装运时付清？

A：Yes, I think that's what we stipulated.

B：请给我点儿时间，让我查一下我的记录。

（B 查阅谈判记录）

A：Right?

B：对的。

A：Would you like to sign the contract now?

B：好的。我在哪里签字？

A：On the last page. We'll sign two originals, each in the Chinese and English language. Both are equally effective.

B：好的。行了吗？

A：Yes. I'm glad our negotiation has come to a successful conclusion.

B：我希望这是我们进一步合作的开端。那我们现在应该握手了。

A：OK. Let's go out and have a drink to congratulate ourselves.

B：好主意！

Chapter 7　Business Etiquette　商务礼仪
口译主题：参观访问

Dialogue 1

1.1

A：明天我们参观哪些地方？

B：Here's a copy of the itinerary of our tour. According to our plan, we will visit the Development Area tomorrow morning.

A：下午呢？

B：In the afternoon we'll go to the downtown area.

A：好的。明早几点出发？

B：I'll come to your hotel at 8:00 to pick you up and we'll set out at 8:30. Is that OK?

A：好的。整个行程多久？

B：Let me see. About 9 or 10 hours. We'll try to get back by 6:00 p.m.

1.2

A：How do you like this itinerary?

B：总的来说不错，能否做点小小的变化调整？

A：Certainly. What changes would you like to make?

B：能否安排去参观一下工厂？

A：OK, we can arrange that. How about the day after tomorrow?

B：好的，谢谢。

A：My pleasure.

Dialogue 2

A：广州开发区位于广州的哪个位置？

B：Guangzhou Development District lies in the east of Guangzhou. It enjoys priority in the development of Guangzhou in recent years.

A：为什么能有这么重要的地位？

B：The fundamental strategy of Guangzhou developing the metropolis areas is "exploration in the south, optimization in the north, extension in the east and co-ordination in the west". Guangzhou Development District, as the center of

Answers for Reference 口译练习参考答案

Guangzhou's eastern area, is the main economic growth area and the major force promoting industrialization and urbanization of Guangzhou.

A: 广州开发区有多大?

B: Guangzhou Development District comprises four adjacent zones and they are: Guangzhou Economic & Technological Development District, Guangzhou Hi-Tech Industrial Development Zone, Guangzhou Export Processing Zone and Guangzhou Free Trade Zone. They were all state-level economic development districts approved by the State Council and began joint administration and operation in 2002.

A: 四合一,这很特别呀!

B: You're right. Such a "four in one" model of administration brings to us unique competitive advantages.

A: 能详细介绍一下吗?

B: Sure. Our major competitive advantages are: a simple and efficient administrative structure, availability to all different investment modes and projects, advantageous geographic location in the Pearl River Delta and well-developed infrastructure.

A: 看来是个宜商宜居的好地方啊。

B: Surely it is. We're striving to build it into a comprehensive manufacturing base, a hi-tech development and production center, a service industry zone with well-developed transportation and logistics infrastructure and an eco-friendly area for living.

Dialogue 3

A: I'll show you around and explain the operation as we go along.

B: 那太好了。

A: That is our office block. We have all the administrative departments there. Down there is the R&D section.

B: 你们每年在研发上花多少钱?

A: About 3%-4% of the gross sales.

B: 对面那座建筑是什么?

A: That's the warehouse. We keep a stock of the faster moving items so that urgent orders can be met quickly from stock.

B: 如果我现在订购,到交货前需要多长时间?

A: It would largely depend on the size of the order and items you want. Well, here we're at the production shop. Put on the helmet, please.

B: 好的。

A: Now please watch your step.

B: 谢谢。生产线都是全自动的吗?

A: Well, not fully-automated.

B: 哦,那你们如何控制质量呢?

A: All products have to go through five checks in the whole manufacturing process.

B: 月产量多少?

A: One thousand units per month now. But we'll be making 1,200 units beginning with next year.

B: 每月不合格率通常是多少?

A: About 0.2% in normal operations.

B: 真不错!成品是从那边出来的吧?

A: Yes. Shall we take a break now?

B: 谢谢你陪同我参观了整个工厂。这次参观让我对你们的产品有了一个很好的了解。

A: It's a pleasure to show our factory to our customers. What's your general impression, may I ask?

B: 很好,尤其是你们的质量控制。能给我一些你们的产品册子吗?如有可能,还有价格表。

A: Sure. Here is our sales catalog and literature.

B: 谢谢。

Chapter 8　Shopping in China　购物口译
口译主题:在中国购物

Dialogue 1

A: 我想买些中国的纪念品送给朋友。

B: You can choose some Chinese crafts, such as cloisonné, pottery, porcelain or jadeware.

A: 另外我还要给我女儿买些礼物,你建议买什么好?

B: I suggest you buy something typically Chinese.

A: 好的,你推荐买什么?

B: How about this jade bracelet?

A: 很漂亮,我买了。这里的特产是什么?

B: Well, I would name chinaware. One of the cities here—Jingdezhen—is famous for chinaware, and it's called the capital of chinaware.

A：太好了，我正好有个朋友喜欢收集瓷器。我给他买几件。

B：OK. Let's select some.

A：我很喜欢这里的女孩打的雨伞。

B：Why not buy one? I'm sure it'll constantly remind you of your visit to this city.

A：哪一把好呢？

B：I think the purple one with Chinese embroidery is great.

Dialogue 2

A：请问去哪里可以买些中国传统的工艺品给我的朋友？

B：You may go to an arts-and-crafts shop if you want to buy some. There is one near the hotel.

A：我们现在就去吗？

B：OK. I guess you want to find something typical Chinese, but not very dear. Am I right?

A：是的。你有什么建议？

B：Well. How about the cloisonné necklace?

A：我不知道我太太是否喜欢。

B：I bet she will. I think a cloisonné necklace would be quite unique as a present.

A：你不觉得这种项链有点老式？

B：No, it's the latest style. Don't you think it's elegant?

A：嗯，我想也许有其他更好的东西。还有什么推荐我买的？

B：How about sandalwood fans? They smell fragrant and refreshing.

A：噢，对了，我听说过这种扇子。帮我鉴别一下真假吧。

B：Yes. A real sandalwood fan has a natural fragrant smell, while the smell of a false one is sort of strong because the scent is added.

A：这些扇子都是同一样式的吗？

B：No. Look, they're of different shapes and sizes. There're square, round and leaf-shaped ones.

A：这把叶形的檀香扇多少钱？

B：100 RMB.

A：与其他类型的一个价钱吗？

B：No. The prices differ with size and design.

Dialogue 3

A：Look, we have a wide variety of Chinese antiques.

B：是的，而且都很漂亮。

A：Is there anything that caters to your taste?

B：嗯，我对中国画很感兴趣。有没有什么好的？

A：Yes, we have plenty of them. Are you looking for anything special?

B：有的。我想要几幅带有本地风情的中国画。

A：How about this picture of cranes with pine trees?

B：噢，我很喜欢。

A：Would you like to buy original paintings or reproductions?

B：请先给我看看原作。

A：OK, here you are. Please take your time.

Dialogue 4

A：我听说中国的丝绸以其设计精良、质量上乘而闻名，在哪里可以买到？

B：It's available in the silk department at any big shopping center.

A：我们去看看好吗？

B：Yes, I'll be glad to.

A：真特别，我从未见过这样的东西。

B：Yes, silk looks brilliant and feels smooth.

A：丝绸一般用来做什么？

B：It can be used to make cheongsam, handkerchief, blouse and so on.

A：旗袍？！那可是很有中国特色的！哪种丝绸适合做旗袍？

B：Something thick and durable would be best.

A：这种丝绸可以水洗吗？

B：Yes. It has been specially treated by a special technique. It will not shrink.

A：我很喜欢，只是有点贵。有没有便宜点的？

B：I can ask them, but generally speaking, a higher price means better quality.

A：你说得对，可我还是觉得贵了点。他们可不可以给我打个折？

B：They say you can enjoy 10% off if you spend more than 300 yuan in the store.

Chapter 9　Seeing Guests Off　送客礼仪
口译主题：送客道别

Dialogue 1

A：时间过得真快！我很快就要回美国了。我很喜欢这次中国之行。

B：I'm planning a farewell dinner for you.

A：谢谢你！非常感谢你在我中国之行中给予的帮助。

B：My pleasure. Let's drink to our friendship. Cheers!

A：干杯！中国菜真好吃，我会想念的。

B：Then help yourself to some more. I'm very glad that you enjoyed your stay here. Please accept this little present as a souvenir from China.

A：哇，真漂亮！非常感谢！

B：I hope it can remind you of your happy tour in China.

A：我肯定会的。

B：Have you finished your packing yet?

A：好了，我可以出发了。

B：OK. Would you please check your passport, ticket and luggage?

A：好的。出租车到了，我们走吧。

B：OK. Let me help you with your luggage.

Dialogue 2

A：你们这儿的海关有什么特别的手续吗？

B：Not really. You just need to show them your passport, China departure card and some customs forms.

A：这里要填哪些表格？

B：Usually you need to show your Customs declaration and currency declaration. You can ask the Customs officers for the forms.

A：关税申报是怎样的程序？

B：You should first fill out the declaration form. You should fill in the form for your foreign currencies, gold, silver and other valuables.

A：如果没有什么要申报的，在哪儿通关？

B：If you have nothing to declare, you can go through the green channel.

A：我给朋友买了些礼物，需要报关税吗？

B：It depends. Tourists are allowed to take out a limited amount of gifts.

A：我买了些丝绸制品，要交关税吗？

B：How much did they cost?

A：大约500元。

B：You're allowed 800 yuan duty free, so you don't have to pay for them.

A：翡翠项链呢？

B：Well, it's not duty free. I'm afraid you'll have to pay quite a tax for it.

A：那我买的中国古画要交税吗？

B：Oh, it's from the Qing Dynasty. It can be taken out of the country without paying any duty.

A：中国画都可以免税吗？

B：Not quite. The export of paintings before the Qing Dynasty is prohibited.

A：我带了点自己抽的烟。

B：I'm afraid you'll have to pay taxes on these things. They exceed the quota.

Dialogue 3

A：道别的时候到了，再次感谢你为我做的一切。

B：It's my pleasure to have been your guide and interpreter. I'm glad I could help.

A：希望我们能再次见面。

B：Me too. Please keep in touch.

A：我在这儿所看到的一切都印象深刻，包括你。

B：Thank you. Do come again!

A：希望你有机会能来美国。

B：I will. Thanks a lot. Have a pleasant journey! Happy landing!

Chapter 10　Cooperation Talks　国际合作
口译主题：教育合作

Dialogue 1

C：I would like to express my gratitude to vice chancellor Pattern and your delegation for joining us in the discussion of the cooperation between our universities.

E：你们能出席本次讨论，我方也感到非常高兴。贵校在中国学生中颇受欢迎，闻名遐迩。我校如能招收贵校的优秀学生，将是我校的莫大荣幸。

C：Then let's get straight to business. I learned from the memorandum that your school will open three-year courses for our students. I am afraid that three-year diploma courses will not be competitive enough. Do you have undergraduate and postgraduate programs available?

E：这一文凭项目可以提供学生升读硕士的机会。就读本项目的学生在大三的时候可以有两种选择。一是登记入读当地的一所大学，然后继续本科的学习，二是出国，在我们学院有合作项目的大学里攻读硕士。

C：All right. Your institute stands out among others. On the one hand, the foreign

universities and colleges acknowledge the diploma and approve our program students have the opportunity to continue their higher study in some of the best institution domestically.

E：我们确实就是这样做的，而且我们觉得这样做能为学生打开多扇门，创造更多的机会。

C：Now, let's discuss whether "1 + 2" or "2 + 2" is better for both of us. I am looking forward to your insights.

E：我觉得"1 + 2"比"2 + 2"要好，因为这能省去学生一年的学费。多一年的学费就可能对一些不是很富裕的家庭造成影响、甚至会吓跑他们。此外，我觉得 4 年时间来完成一个专科项目太长了。据我了解，很多中英合作的大学计划都是以"1 + 2"甚至是"1 + 1"的模式来合作的。

C：Indeed, "1 + 2" mechanism saves money and time for students, but I am worried that one year's preparation will not be sufficient for students to get ready for the overseas study? Would they feel uncomfortable and not fit in after the hasty preparation?

E：所以我们要求学生在中国所上的课有一半是由我方的教员来授课，另外一半则由贵方的教师来授课。我们觉得这样可以为学生在语言、学习方式、英国习俗等各方面做好准备。

C：When it comes to the overseas teacher, the teaching quality concerns many parents, so can you briefly tell us about the teaching team in your college?

E：教师队伍是该项目最根本的优势。我们有非常积极、有实力的教师资队伍。他们深信教育机构所传授的知识将影响学生的未来。

C：How about the English Language teachers and the Business teachers? They are of greatest concerns.

E：我们的英语外教要求具有教学经验，愿意为学生提供学习上的帮助。商务外教不仅要求具有教育背景，还需要至少四年的工作经验。

C：Good! With the teaching quality is assured, we are confident to deliver the "1 + 2" mechanism.

E：太好了！我们把剩下的细节留待下次会议再讨论吧？我觉得今天已经取得了不少成果。

Dialogue 2

C: Among the many counties, why should we single out U.K. as the destination to study English?

B: 英国是英语的故乡,在英国学习能为学生提供了解英国生活与文化的良机。无论你将来的目标是什么,你所习得的语言技能将助你走上成功之路。

C: What advantages do British universities hold to attract more and more overseas students?

B: 英国的教育传统可追溯到数百年前,并一直在改进完善。英国的学历资格得到全世界的认可和尊重,因此,在英国的求学经历将为你的未来奠定坚实的基础。

C: Can you give us a landscape of what British schools look like?

B: 英国的校园气氛活泼生动、富有创新精神和挑战性。在这样的环境里,你能很好地学习并发展自己的潜能。英国学校的质量标准也是世界一流的。学校要不遗余力地证明本校的课程是达到严格的质量标准,因为很多国家在效仿英国,沿用英国设立的标准。

C: What is the learning culture like in UK? Can you outline some of the leaning scenarios?

B: 当然可以!在英国,无论是学习、日常生活、看电视电影还是阅读书报、购物和娱乐,你几乎每时每刻都在练习自己的英语技能。英国全境都说英语,虽然各地的口音和你学习时听到的英语有所不同,不过很快你就能适应过来。

C: The academic atmosphere is internationally renowned. How about the extracurricular activities in the British universities? Are they equally fascinating?

B: 在学校和学院,你有机会参加丰富多彩的休闲活动和社交活动。你可以加入运动队、志愿组织和兴趣小组如,戏剧、音乐、艺术或环保,校方还经常安排去当地的戏剧院、博物馆、旅游景点、运动景点和其他景点参观。

C: Is it very expensive to study in UK? Many parents are digging into the tuition-and-quality balance of a university. They tend to choose Australia, New Zealand and even France as the destination.

B: 英国是英语的故乡,它拥有丰富的历史遗产、参差多态的文化和迷人的社会景象。随着时间的推移,你会越来越了解英国的多元文化,结交到让你终生

铭记的朋友，留下一段难以忘怀的经历。我承认，英国的学费会稍微贵一些，但是这是物有所值的，因为你可以领略古老而纯正的英国文化，而这是无法用价格来衡量的。

C: Now that pounds are depreciated against RMB, will the British side increase the tuition? If so, how much will the British schools bring the tuition up?

B: 在学费方面会涨一点，但我相信中国的家长和学生都能承担这一涨幅。人民币升值后，我相信外国留学生在英国的生活开支会减少，因此他们在学费上不必过虑。

C: It is reported that an increasing number of overseas students are drawn to the British schools. Will the booming quantity affect the quality of teaching? Are you personally concerned with this issue?

B: 我们决不会以任何借口而降低质量标准。英国的大学一贯享有优秀的教学和科研传统。即使有越来越多的学生来英国，我们仍设定了一个标准，我们决不会仅仅为了要更多的学生而降低这个标准。

Dialogue 3

J: 孔子学院的办学宗旨是什么？

R: Confucius Institutes are non-profit language institutions whose mission is to enhance understanding of the Chinese language and culture by people around the world, to deepen friendly relationships between China and other nations, to promote the development of multiculturalism and to build a harmonious world.

J: 你能给我们分享一下有关孔子的数据吗？例如，有多少所是已经在办学？有多少所正在筹备中？

R: By the end of 2007, 210 Confucius Institutes, inclusive of Confucius Classrooms, have been established in 64 countries and regions around the world. A total of 125 Institutes have started offering programs and 85 are in preparation.

J: 在北京孔子学院总部，日常的工作范围有哪些？

R: First of all, the headquarter has put forward a series of regulations and bylaws. Secondly, in the recruitment of Chinese directors and instructors, a strict screening process has been taken to ensure high quality. Thirdly, measures have been taken to publish and promote the usage of textbooks in multi-languages and multi-media teaching resources. Fourthly, new Chinese test programs have been developed and launched; test question design and test administration have been improved. Fifthly, efforts have been made to raise funds in order to further increase financial support from the Chinese side to the Confucius Institutes. The total input by the Headquarters has reached US $26 million in 2006.

J: 孔子学院的办学特色有哪些?

R: We have several measures at hand. Confucius Institutes have open up to communities by providing non-degree Chinese classes. The institutes also play a leading role in promoting Chinese language teaching in primary and secondary schools. What's more important, some of the institutes start degree education where they offer classes featuring Chinese culture and organized a variety of cultural activities.

J: 大家都对中国文化特色课程很感兴趣,你能否举例介绍一下。

R: We normally tailor the classes to the interests of local community. We have a variety of courses, such as Chinese medicine regimen, martial arts, shadowboxing, Shaolin Boxing, Peking Opera, and even introduction to Beijing Olympic Games.

J: 到孔子学院求学的典型人群有哪些?

R: Civil servants, company staff, retired people, drivers, guides, students and businessmen. They come to Confucius Institute either out of their own interests in Chinese culture or out of the working requirements.

J: 中方参与到孔子学院是一项互惠互利的合作项目,你能否举些例子来说明这一点?

R: Beijing Foreign Studies University, China had sent 25 deans of departments, key teachers, and volunteers to help 11 universities in 9 countries establish Confucius Institutes. This has not only helped Chinese language learning abroad but also provided teachers and students of non-English majors good opportunities to practice their foreign languages in native environments. Reciprocally, the Confucius Institute at the University of Rome La Sapienza, Italy sent teachers of Latin to teach at Beijing Foreign Studies University.

J: 你觉得今后孔子学院的办学会有什么新的特色?

R: The Confucius Institute should entail three centers, namely promotion centers, teaching and training centers, and exam and research centers. This will enable the local communities to learn Chinese and sustain the enthusiasm of knowing about China.

Chapter 11　Dealing with Cultural Differences
文化差异的处理
口译主题：文化交流

Dialogue 1

R: With two other hit shows on GIO featuring strong, complex and conflicted women, do you feel pressure to develop the female characters on the show in order to appeal to female viewers?

D: GIO 制作室在人物刻画方面已更上一层楼，不管是男性角色还是女性角色。因此，很自然我们希望我们的角色能达到观众的期望。我们的剧本作家在塑造角色方面做得很出色，而我们的演员都在用心去演，把角色演活了，赋予角色人性的魅力和复杂性。

R: Do you feel pressure to achieve the quality and awards that other GIO films have received?

D: 嗯，我从来都不担心获奖与否，但是我们都感觉到压力，因为我们都想尽可能地制作最好的电影。对于电影制作人而言，这是一项我们都热衷的项目，因此我们都会倾注自己的心血。

R: How will you keep this film from becoming a formula driven plot-based one like *Runway Jury*? Do you plan on developing character-based storylines to intrigue viewers?

D: 我觉得如果我们自始至终都忠于自己的激情，努力实现目标，我们就会有所建树。像我刚才说的，这不仅是我们的一项工作，而是真正的激情。

R: You're known for big blockbuster event movies. Have you considered film-related products? Are the Internet and the opportunity to create an online game part of the project?

D: 其实，这都是讲故事的技巧，不管是在电影、电视、漫画书、游戏、手机或网络上。每一个媒介都有挑战，但是归根到底都是讲述一群人物在旅程征途

上的故事。如果你把故事讲好了，那么就会有收获，不管你用何种媒介来讲。

R: How do you hope the online game will influence viewers?
D: 我希望观众在玩游戏的时候，他们能走进我们人物所生活的世界。也许，这些观众能从一个独特的角度看到这些人物角色如何行事，为什么这样行事。

R: What process did you use in finding the right chemistry and balance for casting the film?
D: 他们的默契是自生自发的。我们去外国拍摄一些外景的时候，演员在镜头外的时间都经常聚在一起，在工作以外的时间，在酒店或出去吃饭都在一起，他们慢慢就拉近了彼此之间的关系，我们都难以预料。到我们开拍整部电影的时候，他们已经默契，我们对此又惊又喜！

Dialogue 2

J: What sets TNT apart from other Shakespeare play groups?
D: 通常，莎士比亚的戏剧都因导演和设计师的强行诠释而扼杀了原作的精粹。TNT剧团努力展现莎士比亚的多姿多彩和博大精深，这种做法受到广大观众的赞赏，他们常常惊叹看到我们上演的纯正莎剧，莎剧变得不再遥不可及。

J: What does TNT do to deliver a Shakespearean play in a way Shakespeare would have intended it?
D: 莎剧的剧本都是适合在有限的场景上演，能焕发出观众的想象力，生动的音乐、为数不多的演员、激情洋溢的表演和诗意般的触觉，所有这些因素都可以在TNT剧团的制作中找到。越不繁，越不凡！

J: Shakespeare as Shakespeare intended it. Why does that work in the 21st century?
D: 把莎翁从众多的顶礼膜拜者中拯救出来，还以莎翁真正的面目：行云流水、富有戏剧性，没有复杂的场景转换，庞大的演员队伍，真实的场景。这样做之所以是可行的，因为本来就该这样做。

J: What is most required of the contemporary audience when watching the Shakespearean plays? Is it necessary to make some preparation before they go to the show? If so, what can they get prepared?
D: 想象力是至关重要的。伊丽莎白时代的观众最大的好处是他们时刻会运用自己的想象力。我们现代的媒体，很遗憾，剥夺了观众的想象力，而我们希望把

这种想象的震撼感带回给观众。观众如果想欣赏莎剧，最好要带上想象力，随着戏剧中诗意的台词而浮想联翩。

J: Why does TNT once again choose Shanghai as the first destination of the China round tour show? Is it because the audiences in Shanghai are passionate and generous?

D: 我想说，我们回到上海是因为观众，在过去几年我们在这里演出的时候，观众和学生们都有很好的反应，我们十分感谢上海的观众，他们很活跃，也很聪明。我们会竭尽所能为他们上演一场感动、振奋、浪漫之夜。

J: Finally, what is it about Shakespeare that is timeless and relevant till today? Why do his plays continue to appeal to the world audience?

D: 答案很简单。莎士比亚是属于全人类的，莎剧超越时空的界限，直奔观众的心灵。莎剧反映了人类社会的永恒主题，因此也感动着我们的每一个人。

Dialogue 3

R: 你小时候的梦想是什么？

D: I wanted to be a painter. I kept painting from my primary school to middle school and remained an active member in the fine art group in the school. Whenever I passed by a cinema, I felt envious of those who were standing on the shelf and painting the poster for movies. I really wanted to be a professional painter for movie posters.

R: 那为什么后来会当编剧呢？

D: In a shooting team, as I observed, artists are merely manual workers. They are bossed around and asked to run errands like replacing chairs and desks with couches. A screen writer, on the contrary, is highly valued by the producers and directors. Back then, screen writers were paid by royalty, which easily out-earned photographers and other artists alike. As I spent enough time in the screen team, I got to know some of the screen writers, and I began to write plays myself.

R: 从编剧到导演这一步容易吗？

D: It was not easy at all. It is not easy to be trusted by people, especially when you are fresh, because a director has a lot to be responsible for, like, the whole team, a large sum of money. Back then, directors were entrusted directly by leaders in the authorities. They usually went for the graduates from institutions of cinemas. To them, I was a mere amateur. But for a screen writer, it was a different story.

Nobody bothers you. You can stay home and write things, if you wish. If you send your manuscripts to the TV production centers or film studios and get recognized, you will be offered a guest room where you could stay and modify the manuscripts.

R：你什么时候开始做导演的？你执导的第一部影片成功吗？

D：My first film under my own directing was in 1997. Back then, I was given a limited amount of money, but I felt blessed, because the film was a great success.

R：在中国，进入影视圈难吗？

D：For those who have just joined the circle, they tend to seek recognitions from the seniors. Bit by bit, one will realize that recognition within the circle is not important, but that from the audience is.

R：那你呢？你自己进入这个圈子难吗？要做哪方面的努力呢？比如不怕受委屈，为人低调，夹着尾巴做人？

D：Of course, personal efforts and perseverance are of more importance. Looking back all those years, I have undergone lots of setbacks. In face of obstacles, some would lose heart and simply quit. They could not bear it. I am different. When injustice is done to me and I feel frustrated, I am able to adjust myself to it. I may be mad in the first place, but I hold the thought that I will definitely accomplish something at the end of the day; you wait and see.

R：作为一个导演，你还有什么样的梦想？

D：I'd like to see more varieties of themes and styles in the Chinese movies. China's market-based economy is developing on the right track, but the cultural circle is still lagging behind. I hope that it will progress rapidly, reform and open up itself. This is a dream I cherish.

R：你怎样看待积极的电影和消极的电影？

D：I must admit that positivity is good, but that does not mean that negativity is bad. When you want to make a movie about a nation, you may feature on the catastrophes that the nation has suffered. In this way, viewers will know more deeply about the nation. The presentation might not be positive, but in a broader sense, it is positive.

Answers for Reference 口译练习参考答案

Chapter 12　Sports Interpreting　体育口译
口译主题：体育活动

Dialogue 1

J：您觉得中国队参加奥运比赛会有怎样的成绩？

P：They have already played one time in Olympics, and another time in world championships. They have some experience. At their age, not a lot of players have those experiences, also they keep improving. I know we have a bigger chance with playing Olympics in home country.

J：您参加雅典奥运会的比赛与参加悉尼奥运会的比赛有什么不同吗？

P：First of all, the Sydney Olympics was my first Olympics. I was very excited that I can be on the team. So naturally, I had more excitement than pressure. I was 20 years old and the youngest player on the team, so all I needed to do was just hustle on the court. And in Athens I was still excited, but I had much more pressures. I had to lead the team, we got into the quarterfinal. We had some success, but also some tough times.

J：您觉得你们在北京奥运会上能取得更佳成绩吗？

P：I really hope so. We should do it.

J：您同时效力NBA和国家队对您有什么特别的意义吗？

P：Playing in the best league in the world has meant a lot to me. It helps me with my skills and my experience. I will try to play on national team so I can help it get better or help keep strong.

J：您觉得奥运会球迷会为国家队疯狂吗？

P：We always get a lot of support from the fans. Basketball is very popular in China. A lot of fans like to play, like to watch a game. And everything we do with the national team, they do like to read the articles, they will watch the TV news, they really care about us.

J：为什么篮球在中国那么流行呢？

P: Because basketball is a fun game, you know! They like to play. They really like to play.

J: 您觉得会有更多的篮球运动员加盟 NBA 吗？

P: Maybe one guy every five years. It's hard to say.

Dialogue 2

R: 当你站在 110 米跨栏起跑线上准备参加奥运会决赛的时候，你脑海里面想到了什么？

A: To be honest, my mind at the time was a complete blank. I wasn't thinking about anything because I already felt like I'd achieved an important breakthrough. Until then, there had never been an Asian in the final of that event in the Olympics, so that was already an accomplishment. I just wanted to make sure I did the best I could, run as fast as I could. That was all I was thinking at the time.

R: 在你冲过终点线的一刹那，你意识到你已经赢了，当时是怎样的感受？

A: As I said, during that entire time, my mind was blank. When I won, everything felt surreal. It's hard to describe. I felt like I was floating, that all my actions and my words... they weren't coming from me. It was like I was watching someone else doing those things, saying those things. I really couldn't express myself because I was too happy and excited. I couldn't take in everything that was going on. It was as if the whole world had turned upside down.

R: 你说仿佛乾坤颠倒了，乾坤确实为运动员而颠倒，你冲破了障碍，而且一位亚洲选手在奥运短跑赛事上胜出，你觉得这代表什么？你觉得此刻的历史重要意义有多大？

A: It was important because in the past, the Europeans and Americans used to think that Asians weren't good enough to succeed in track and field events, that we weren't a threat, especially in the men's events. And we used to think that because we're Chinese, track and field wasn't something we could do. So I think that by winning, I bring credits to Asian athletes.

R: 你觉得你的胜出会影响到下一代中国运动员来追随你的步伐吗？

A: With my win, I hope I can encourage others, and tell them that no matter what obstacles they face, whatever difficulties there are, all they need is to work hard and

face the challenges head on. Challenges are meant to be met and overcome. Everyone can do it!

R：你牺牲了多少？你为了赢得金牌付出了多少？

A：Honestly, training is very tough. It's only when you get used to it that it's not so bad. You just have to give whatever it takes and be the best because this is your profession. I feel like I've been very fortunate to have won a gold medal at the Olympics.

R：据说赢得金牌就像赢得一百万美元那样，因为赞助会让你变得富有。那么你觉得自己很快就会变得富裕吗？

A：I feel that often in life, material satisfaction is inferior to spiritual satisfaction. You just cannot compare the feeling of being emotionally fulfilled. That's really what I think. If a person has too much money, then money is just about numbers. It's actually very simple—if you perform well and get good results, you will get rewarded. That's the way it works. At the moment, I think that among my peers, I consider myself a rich man. But I still think that spiritual wealth is so much more important than material wealth.

R：说到物质生活，据说你很喜欢唱，而且唱得很好。你打算以后唱歌吗，或者会推出唱片吗？

A：I just sing karaoke with family and friends, when I want to relax. But it's only for entertainment! My singing is only at the amateur level. I'm definitely not good enough to sing in public. It's not what I'm good at. What I'm good at is track!

R：最后，我想问的是你觉得会有什么比赢得金牌更胜一筹的吗？你觉得以后的生活会有什么能跟赢得金牌相媲美吗？

A：I'm sure that there must be something better out there, but life is unpredictable. And I don't know what will happen to me after I retire, so as long as I have dreams I will continue to try to realize them.

Dialogue 3

R：Tieshan Football Club is still strange to us. Could you please introduce this Club to us?

S：铁山足球还没真正参加联赛。但目前俱乐部已经初具规模，也有一些有实力的球员。我们国内联赛水平很高的，我们需要吸引更多的球员，邀请更多球员充实我们的实力。

R: Could you tell us something about your coach team, the contract term and payment, if this is not an impertinent question.

S: 沙朗教练会来帮我忙，他是我在法国时候的助理教练，我们彼此都非常熟悉了。另外的教练我们还会再找。这是我第一次在中国带比赛，我还需要摸索，一步一步地去组建我们的球队。

R: You have been quite successful in coaching football teams. Each team you coached would be successful. But now given that you are in charge of a completely newly-built team, do you feel any pressure?

S: 我虽然有很多成功的经验，但在中国足球联赛方面我却是从零开始，这是我第一次执教中国俱乐部。希望国内的朋友和同行能够一起努力，把中国足球联赛的水平提高上去。我非常期待这样的工作。

R: Why did you choose to come to China to coach?

S: 两方面原因！第一，我觉得中国足球的发展仍有很大的空间，所以我想为中国足球发展做点儿贡献。另外，我非常希望能积累更多的执教经验，因为我自己已经在欧洲和美洲执教过了，所以很自然地想到亚洲的国家，而这时候铁山俱乐部恰好联系了我，我就来了。

R: You are a well-known figure in the international football community. Now you are to coach a Chinese local team. Has it occurred to you that you are a big fish in a small pool?

S: 人各有志吧，我非常喜欢足球事业，希望大家能从关注我到关注我带的中国队伍。其实中国的政策、资金投入各方面都很好，绝对没有委屈的感觉。

R: Could you comment on the Tieshan Club?

S: 铁山有一个很好的基础，管理得十分好。我跟各管理人员、球员之间的沟通也很好。我相信铁山会是全国联赛的一匹黑马。

R: What kinds of players are you expecting to recruit?

S: 我接下来会联系一些我们需要的球员。一些本土的球员会因年纪稍大而退役，我们考虑会招募他们。同时我们也会从国际上邀请一些球员来中国。我以前

所带的一些不错的球员也在考虑之列。

R：You mentioned that you liked China. What exactly do you like China about?

S：现在的中国是个非常开放和包容性很强的国家，我在中国生活和工作很荣幸，中国饮食也非常出名，我很喜欢中国悠久的文化历史。

Chapter 13　Diplomatic Interpreting　政治外交口译
口译主题：政治访问

Dialogue 1

C：Welcome to Guangzhou, Mr. Smith. First of all, please allow me, on behalf of Guangzhou Municipal Government, to extend my warmest Guangdong welcome to you and your delegation. Did you enjoy your flight?

E：我们坐了14个小时的飞机从美国来到中国，然后又乘了1个小时的汽车才到这里。旅途漫长，我们都有点累了，但您的热情让我们精神焕发，像回到家一样倍感亲切。

C：That's great. China is known as a country of courtesy and Chinese people are very hospitable to guests. An ancient Chinese saying goes "It is such a delight to have friends from afar." Now you have traveled to Guangzhou from the other side of Pacific Ocean, so you are our guests of honor. We are most happy to welcome all of you.

E：谢谢您的盛情款待。我们代表团对您和您带领的所有工作人员表示衷心的感谢，谢谢你们的招待！

C：It's my pleasure. Mr. Smith, if my memory serves, your last visit was five years ago, wasn't it?

E：确实是啊！您记性真好！自从我上次访问广州以后，我一直期待着我下一次还能到访广州，今天我终于成行了。

C：Your visit 5 years ago prompted the twin cities relation, and I sincerely hope that your current visit will be even more fruitful for the benefits of people of our two cities.

E：谢谢您的夸奖。上次的到访确实是非常成功，我也期望本次的到访能为我们两市带来更多的便利。我们打算会见来自企业、生产工厂、销售代理、医药

公司的代表和外贸官员。

C: I believe that your current visit will create many trade and business opportunities for us. Speaking of which, are you planning to pay a visit to Canton Fair?

E: 在上次的访问期间,我已经去了广交会。这次,我们代表团的一些成员会抽空到广交会的展览馆看看。我听说广交会的会址换地方了,对吧?

C: Yes. In the 104th session, the Canton Fair entered a new era of development marked by "New Complex, New Phase, New Opportunities": the Canton Fair was completely moved into the Pazhou Complex, adopting a significant reform of 3 phases in 1 session. This has led to many encouraging outcomes. Take the 105th session as an example, 21,709 exhibitors participated in the export hall and 395 exhibitors in the import hall, with a business turnover of 26.23 billion USD.

E: 广交会成绩斐然,我对此印象深刻。毫无疑问,我们代表团成员到广交会参观肯定会有所收获。

C: Since our two cities have established the twin relationship, the trade volume has increased at an annual rate of 5.7%. As you will be meeting representatives from the industrial and commercial circles, and visiting the Canton Fair, I am sure that the trade volume between our two cities will be even greater.

E: 我对此十分同意。

C: Finally, I sincerely hope that the twin cities will see a closer tie and better life for our people.

E: 谢谢您,市长阁下! 我想借此机会向市长阁下发出邀请,请阁下尽早到我们美丽的城市参观访问,让我们能答谢您今天对我们的盛情款待。

C: Thank you for your kind invitation. I shall go and visit your beautiful hometown as soon as possible.

E: 太好了! 再见!

Dialogue 2

W: I would like to offer my warmest welcome to honourable Mr. Louis Sean for your visit to our Bureau. Over the past years, our Bureau and EPA have been discussing the issues of environmental protection, energy and climate change. We have reached

many censuses, which I am sure serve as solid foundation for today's deliberation.

L: 我非常高兴看到我们两个部门能在环保议题上取得那么多的成绩。其实，在环保这一崇高的事业上，我们还有很多的空间可以开展积极的合作。

W: Thank you for your acknowledgment of our work. You mentioned that we have more room to engage cooperation. May I ask you to elaborate on this topic and share your insights with us?

L: 好的，我们首先要继续进行战略经济对话，尤其在清洁能源和气候变化问题上。我们可以探讨两国合作发展清洁能源的机会。而且我们应发展由双方的研究人员共同设计执行的专利技术产品的机制。

W: I agree with you. We should stick to the 10-year cooperation framework in environmental protection, energy, and climate change within the strategic economic dialogue framework.

L: 是的，我们应在《中美能源环境十年合作框架》的基础上进一步扩大双方的合作。我很高兴看到中国政府在哥本哈根气候峰会上所作的必要努力，我相信中国的经济和政策会对减排作出更大的贡献。

W: That's for sure. We should strive for a closer cooperation tie. In the space of 20 years, that's from 1980 to 2000, the energy efficiency has been doubled. As is stipulated in the eleventh five year plan, by the year of 2010, the energy consumption per unit GDP will decrease by 20%. It is clear that Chinese government is firm in resolution to tackle the climate change and environmental protection.

L: 中国政府所作的努力是值得称赞的，同时也体现了中国国家领导人对环境保护的重视。我相信对中国的可持续发展大有可为。

W: It is reported that, by 2020, developed countries are required to reduce the greenhouse gas emission from 25% to 40% against the 1990 level. As one of the officers from the environmental agencies, do you feel stressed to meet this target?

L: 我认为技术上这一目标是可以实现的。我部现在致力于建设现代化电网，鼓励绿色建筑及设计，改造各政府的办公大楼，实现高能效。我们还倡导国民贯彻"三用"原则（即减少使用、重复使用、循环使用），使用可再生能源，并且让民众在观念上变得更节能。

W: As far as public education is concerned, I am sure you have achieved fairly good results. Can you share with us your experience in this regards?

L: 我们应该教育民众在日常的生活中，尽可能多地考虑环境的影响。譬如说我们应多用紧凑型荧光灯，不用白炽灯。我们开展宣传教育运动，介绍垃圾分类等常识。关键是让民众意识到，生活中的小细节对环保的贡献也是巨大的。

W: Yes. In China, we have similar gesture to serve that purpose. Starting from 1st June of last year, shops, supermarkets and sales outlets would be forbidden to offer free plastic bags and people have to pay for a plastic bag if they wish to use it. This mandatory policy is to prevent the "white pollution" from deterioration and better curb the environmental degradation.

L: 我也听说了这一举措，我觉得这是中国政府一项非常好的措施，从生活做起，从而让中国人的生活变得更绿色，更有利于可持续发展。我希望中国各级政府能自始至终贯彻相关政策，不要重蹈美国的覆辙。

W: What do you mean by "repeating the American mistakes"?

L: 在美国历史上，当油价很贵的时候，大家都倡导使用节油的汽车，但是当油价便宜的时候，人们就渐渐淡忘了，开始使用大耗油量的汽车。我希望中国不要重蹈覆辙，在经济发展和环境保护上取得平衡。

W: I fully subscribe myself to your view and I am delighted that you have followed so closely with our endeavours. Finally, I want to express my heartfelt thanks for your visit.

Dialogue 3

A: First and foremost, we would like to express our special welcome to you, Mr. Ambassador. And thank you for your acceptance of having this interview. Our first question goes as follows: You assumed the office as the Swiss Ambassador to China last year and what strikes you most ever since then?

E: 令我感受最深的是中国人民对未来经济的乐观和自信。世界各地都受到金融危机的威胁，这些地区当然包括欧洲、美国和亚洲。但是我在中国看到更多的是中国人民对发展更强大的经济所具有的决心，尽管有经济危机。

A: You have served as Switzerland Ambassador to Thailand, Myanmar, Laos and Cambodia and you are now the Switzerland Ambassador in China. Do you think this

Answers for Reference 口译练习参考答案

is a new challenge in your diplomatic career?

E：我之前在这些国家任职，为我在中国任职打下了基础。但我还想说，东南亚和中国是不一样的。我发现中国人的表达更直接；在处理人际关系的时候，更务实。

A：Earlier this year, during Premier Wen Jiabao's Journey of Confidence to Europe, Switzerland was the first country he visited. How do you comment on this gesture?

E：温总理能够来访瑞士，我们非常高兴。欧盟并不能代表整个欧洲，在欧洲还有很多国家没有加入欧盟。瑞士就是非欧盟的国家之一，而瑞士也是第一批承认中华人民共和国的国家。所以，温总理选择瑞士作为欧洲之旅的第一站是恰当不过的。

A：In the bilateral relationship between our countries, trade relationship is very important. Statistics show that in the year of 2007, the Sino-Swiss trade volume registered a hiking increase and Switzerland experienced trade surplus to China. Can you account for the surplus situation for us?

E：确实如您所说，在过去几年，瑞士对中国的贸易是有顺差的。中国现在是瑞士在亚洲最大的贸易伙伴。为什么会有这个顺差？因为中国和瑞士两国的出口产品有很大的互补性，瑞士除了向中国出口一些传统的奢侈品，比如说手表以外，还向中国出口高科技的机械产品。

A：Speaking of the financial and trade, we are noted that the China Securities Regulatory Commission has rectified the joint venture co-funded by a Chinese security company and Credit Suisse. This joint venture is regarded as the "Happy Marriage" between the two sides. What do you think of it?

E：在我看来，这家合资公司会为中国市场和中国内地的投资者提供更多的投资机会。当中方的企业家在合资公司里做决定的时候，他们可以借鉴瑞士合伙人的经验。我很高兴看到在金融合作领域，我们两国逐渐融合。我觉得我们现在是在双行道上，不是在单行道上，我们最终会取得双赢的结果。

A：Switzerland is known as a permanent neutral country. Could you explain to us what a "neutral country" is?

E：瑞士之所以是中立国是由历史和地理因素造成的。瑞士的邻邦都是大国，所以早在16、17世纪的时候，瑞士就决定不参加任何的战争。"中立"就意味着你不加入任何联盟或军事条约。

161

A: Given the complicated international diplomatic relationship, how can you ensure neutrality in the foreign affairs?

E: 保持中立,并不意味着在表达观点的时候就要保持缄默。中立仅仅意味着不加入任何军事联盟或条约。因为加入了联盟后,一旦发生冲突,你就不能置身于冲突之外了。例如,我们绝不会为了获得更安全或更多军事的保障而加入北约等类似的组织。

A: As we all know, Geneva is a favoured choice as a headquarter picked by many international organisations. Does this have anything to do with the neutrality of Switzerland?

E: 我觉得是有关系的。我觉得这一偏好从国家联盟的时候就开始了,国联即是现在联合国的前身。瑞士的中立加上其他的特点,如谨慎、尊重国际组织的独立性,都促使越来越多的国际组织选择瑞士作为总部。

A: Thank you very much, Mr. Ambassador, for your kind answers to our questions regarding China and Switzerland. At the very end of our program, what do you have to say to our TV viewers?

E: 我想对中国朋友说,虽然瑞士面积不大,人口不多,但是瑞士是中国的重要伙伴。瑞中两国在很多问题上都有共同的关切。因为我们两国的经济有很强的互补性,而且两国领导人都相互尊重,我们可以发展更紧密的关系,而我也会尽我所能,使两国的关系朝着更密切的合作方向发展。

A: Thank you very much, Mr. Ambassador. We sincerely hope that you have a nice and happy stay in China.

Chapter 14　Medical Service Interpreting　医疗服务口译
口译主题:中医中药

Dialogue 1

F: 我对中医十分着迷。我在美国的时候,有人跟我说针灸对病人来说像魔术一样,因此今天我特意来多了解一下中医。

D: Thank you for your interests and trust in our traditional medicine and its culture. Acupuncture is famous for its special effects for diseases like high blood pressure, tension, and injuries in sports.

Answers for Reference 口译练习参考答案

F: 太神奇了。最近我一直为考试而忐忑不安，您觉得针灸能帮我缓解压力吗？

D: That's for sure. Acupuncture is performed to tap into the specific points in your body, thus striking a balance of Qi, the energy, within and relaxing your body and mind.

F: 对了，我经常听到"气"这一字眼。我对此十分好奇，您能给我多讲几句吗？

D: In TCM theory, Qi is regarded as the vital force of life. The well-being of a person is influenced by the flow of Qi.

F: 我以为气是指空气，现在知道气是指体内的能量了。另外，我有点担心，针灸要用针扎进体内，这会不会不安全？

D: Please rest assured that it is safe. Acupuncture does not mean that needles will be inserted into your body randomly. Needles are inserted into the specific points of your body. Besides, acupuncture needles are tiny and thin. As long as the expertise of the acupuncture practitioners is guaranteed, you feel that the pain is relieved, rather than feeling hurt.

F: 听了以后我可以放心了。我想马上就试一下针灸，还是我先要预约？

D: I am afraid it is not available now. Appointments must be booked beforehand. How about coming around at 10 a.m. the day after tomorrow?

F: 后天10点吗？恐怕我不行，因为那天我有其他事情。周五下午3点怎样？

D: Fine. No problem!

F: 还有一件事情，我的中国朋友说我这几天上火了？什么是"上火"呢？

D: "Excessive internal heat" is believed as a heat syndrome by TCM.

F: 您说的热证是不是发烧的意思？

D: Fever is just one of the symptoms. But that isn't the syndrome of excessive internal heat. There are several causes leading to the excessive internal heat: heart fire, liver fire, stomach fire, and lung fire. Each one has different symptoms.

F: 那我们应该怎样下火呢？听上去，中医都成了消防员。

D: Generally speaking, bitter things or things with high water content are cooling foods that may help you get rid of the excessive internal heat.

F: 今天我学了很多东西。在周五我的第一次针灸预约，咱们再见。
D: See you then!

Dialogue 2

D: Good morning. I assume you feel much better after the acupuncture treatment?
F: 好多了。谢谢！我没有觉得很大压力了。针灸的确很棒。

D: So what can I do for you today?
F: 是的。我今天来是想更详细了解一下中国传统医学，或简称中医。针灸的疗效让我着迷不已，于是我开始对古老的中国疗法和药物倍感兴趣。你能不能给我讲一下其中的奥妙？

D: Yes, Traditional Chinese Medicine has a history of more than 5,000 years. It has a complete set of theories about the cause, development and treatment of diseases. Acupuncture is only one of the common ways to treat diseases.

F: 除此以外，我对中医还是不甚了解。你能否多给我讲点？
D: No problem. It is the belief of TCM that the cause of diseases is the imbalance between Yin and Yang and to cure diseases is to restore the balance between them.

F: 嗯，上次我们谈到"气"。如果我没有记错的话，"气"即能量。那么什么是阴和阳呢？
D: Yes, that's right. Qi means energy. As to Yin and Yang, they are two concepts from ancient Chinese philosophy and they represent the binary oppositions in everything. In TCM theory, Yin and Yang are two concepts to explain physiological and pathological phenomena of the body. They are also the guiding principles of diagnosing and curing diseases.

F: 那么你们中医师是怎样用这一理论来给病人治病的呢？
D: Generally speaking, when dealing with diseases, there are two common ways of TCM treatments: medicinal treatment and non-medicinal treatment.

F: 药物治疗通常都用什么药？而非药物治疗又是怎样的呢？
D: As for medicinal treatment, traditional Chinese medicines are made from herbs, minerals, animals, etc. As for non-medicinal treatment, there are acupuncture,

massage, cupping, scrapping and so on.

F: 关于针灸和按摩，我现在有了一些肤浅的了解。拔火罐是怎么回事？

D: It is a congested treatment using a vacuum cup suctioned firmly to the skin. Usually, the doctor would light up an alcohol sponge and puts it inside the cup for a short while to vacuum the cup. Then he immediately places the vacuum cup over the selected body surface.

F: 我听说过灸法，它与针法和拔火罐类似吗？

D: Moxibustion is a therapeutic procedure involving ignited material, usually moxa, to apply heat to certain points or areas of the body surface for curing disease through regulation of the function of meridians and visceral organs.

F: 非常感谢！我现在对中医的理解又加深了。

Dialogue 3

A: The conflicts between TCM and WM have been waging for years in China. Professor, could you introduce the features of WM to us? What is the difference between TCM and WM?

P: 西医以科学方法著称，关注可测量的生化过程。西医把所有医药现象看成是因果的关系，并依靠药物、放射、手术等来减轻症状，治愈疾病。与之相对，中医着重全面的治疗，把宇宙与人体用哲学的高度来把握。例如，阴阳均衡有助养"气"，气乃是万物生命之本。

A: Then, how are TCM and WM perceived by the consumers?

P: 消费者认为中医药效比较慢，副作用比较温和，并更注重潜在疾病的治理，而不是减缓病征。另外，当消费者不清楚自身的情况而又不急于解决的话，他们会倾向于选择中医。西医对于消费者来说则是治标不治本的。

A: Well, is it possible that consumers will be doubtful of the soundness of TCM, because of its slow effect?

P: 冰冻三尺，非一日之寒。我们也不要指望中医师能在短时间内完全治愈我们的健康问题。对于已到疾病晚期的病人，我还是建议他们采取西医作为短期的治疗方式，而中医作为后备的长期的治疗方式。

A: Many people denounce that TCM is of no scientific grounding and that the prescriptions and treatments of TCM are based on wild guesses. Do you agree?

P: 对此观点,恕我难以同意。事实上,中医的科学根据在国际范围内或多或少都是认可的。例如,世界卫生组织认可针灸是一种有效的治疗方式,并发布了一份清单,涵盖了41种可用针灸治疗的疾病,其中包括:呼吸道疾病,疼痛及慢性痛症,经前综合征和其他妇科疾病,消化系统疾病及其他健康问题。

A: In addition to WHO, is there any other organization that lends support to TCM?

P: 几年前,美国国立卫生研究院出版了其研究发现,对针灸的好处十分认可。报告对针灸的确认疗效和很有可能有疗效进行分类。例如,确认疗效的疾病有:手术后恶心、怀孕期间恶心、牙科手术后疼痛。很有可能有疗效的疾病有:头疼、哮喘、中风后康复。

A: As we are all concerned about the scientific grounding of TCM, could you tell us whether a scientific explanation is available to account for the effects of acupuncture?

P: 事实上,针灸是有科学根据的。针灸可以增加T细胞的数量,从而增强免疫力。这大概可以解释针灸为什么对过敏及慢性疾病的症状有改善的疗效。另外,针灸可以释放有止痛效用的内啡肽。内啡肽对荷尔蒙系统的运作起关键作用。最重要的是,针灸可引导生命之源——"气",在经络的穴位上针灸,有助于平衡体内各主要器官的能量。

A: Is TCM as popular in U.S. as it is in China? Could you tell us what is TCM like in US?

P: 中医在美国十分受欢迎。例如,美国政府资助了100万美元经费,用于研究针灸对戒除上瘾行为的疗效。在纽约、迈阿密、明尼阿波利斯都有资助项目,研究用针灸治疗毒瘾和酗酒的行为。在2000年,美国估计有11 000名认证的针灸治疗师,其数目到2010年将会翻一番。

Chapter 15 Legal Service Interpreting 法律服务口译
口译主题:法律事务

Dialogue 1

F: 您好!一家中国本土的公司跟我接触过,我自己对在中国工作也很感兴趣。因此,我来这里询问一些信息。首先,在中国工作需要满足什么条件?

L: Any foreigner seeking employment in China shall meet the following conditions: (1) One must be 18 years of age or older and in good health; (2) One must be

with professional skills and job experience required for the work of intended employment; (3) One must be with no criminal record; (4) One has a clearly-defined employer; (5) One must have a valid passport or other international travel document in lieu of the passport.

F: 我听说在某些情况下，外籍劳工可免申领就业证和就业许可证，这种说法属实吗？

L: Foreign professional technical and managerial personnel employed directly by the Chinese government or those with senior technical titles or credentials of special skills recognized by their home or international technical authorities or professional associations to be employed by Chinese government organs and institutions and foreigners holding Foreign Expert Certificate issued by China's Bureau of Foreign Expert Affairs may be exempted from the Employment License and Employment Permit.

F: 还有其他情况可以享受这种特别的待遇吗？

L: Foreign workers with special skills who work in offshore petroleum operations without the need to go ashore for employment and hold "Work Permit for Foreign Personnel Engaged in the Offshore Petroleum Operations in the People's Republic of China"; and foreigners who conduct commercialized entertaining performance with the approval of the Ministry of Culture and hold "Permit for Temporary Commercialized Performance".

F: 如果我要申请就业证或就业许可证，我在申请的时候须提交什么文件？

L: You must submit the following documents: (1) the curriculum vitae of the foreigner to be employed; (2) the letter of intention for employment; (3) the report of reasons for employment; (4) the credentials of the foreigner required for the performance of the job; (5) the health certificate of the foreigner to be employed; (6) other documents required by regulations.

F: 劳动合同期限为多久？

L: The employer and its foreign employee should, in accordance with law, conclude a labour contract, the term of which shall not exceed five years. Such contract may be renewed upon expiration after the completion of clearance process in accordance with relevant rules.

F: 没有居住证的外国人（即：持有F，L，C或G类签证）的外国人和在中国学习或短期访问的外国人可以在中国工作吗？

L: No, they can't. In special cases, employment may be allowed when the foreigner changes his status at the public security organs with the Employment License secured by his employer in accordance with the clearance procedures, under these rules foreigners changes his status at the public security organs with the Employment License and receives his Employment Permit and Residence Certificate.

F: 如果居留资格被取消，还能继续就业吗？

L: For foreigner whose residence status is revoked by public security organs due to his violation of Chinese law, his labour contract should be terminated by his employer and his Employment Permit be withdrawn by the labour administrative authorities.

F: 好的。我对相关的规章制度有大概的认识了。谢谢您的帮助。

L: My pleasure!

Dialogue 2

F: 我想在北京购房，需要出示什么证件文书吗？

C: Foreigners who intend to buy a house in Beijing need a certificate issued by the Beijing Municipal Public Security Bureau to prove that they have stayed in China for at least one year for reasons of work or study.

F: 外国居民在中国购买房产需注意什么？

C: Before buying real property, the foreigner should make sure that it meets all governmental or regulatory requirements, proven by a Commodity Housing Sale License or Pre-sale License if the building is unfinished, issued by local government authorities.

F: 签署购买合同的时候，要注意些什么？

C: In case of buying, the buyer and seller usually sign a model commodity-housing buy and sales contract formulated by the local housing administrative bureau. Such a contract usually stipulates standard terms such as the area and price, building and turnover conditions, developer's guarantee and warranties, and future management. In addition, the parties often sign a supplemental agreement containing other specific issues and terms in relation to the transaction.

F：合同的语言是用中文来写的吗？有没有用外国语言写的呢？
C：Contracts are usually written in Chinese. It is advisable that the foreigner request a parallel version of the contract written in his or her own language. Assistance can be available from lawyers in China who are capable of serving their clients in other languages as well as in Chinese.

F：外国居民置业的时候需要到政府部门登记吗？
C：Foreigners should be advised that any buying or selling of real property in China must be registered with the government office in charge of real property and land administration. If not, the transaction is not legitimate, and the rights of the buyer or seller in relation to the property are not sufficiently protected until it has been properly registered and recorded in accordance with Chinese law.

F：置业的时候需要缴付什么税呢？
C：There are taxes and fees that should be paid in relation to transactions. For example, a buyer of a house should pay the contract tax and stamp tax, as well as the registration fees for the property of the house and its underlying land use right.

F：最后一个问题，如果我购置房产后想将其出租，我需要通知有关部门吗？还是我不用知会有关当局就能直接出租？
C：If you want to buy houses to rent or sell or change them for commercial use, you should apply to set up a foreign company and obtain an operations certificate.

Dialogue 3

F：在中国设立中外合资经营企业是否具有法人地位？
C：Sino-foreign equity joint ventures established within China's territory in accordance with the Law on Sino-foreign Joint Ventures are Chinese legal persons and are subject to the jurisdiction and protection of the Chinese law.

F：在中国可以设立何种合营企业呢？
C：Generally speaking, we all support various kinds of joint ventures to set up in China, but applications shall not be granted approval if the project involves any of the following conditions: (1) detriment to China's sovereignty; (2) violation of the Chinese law; (3) nonconformity with the requirements of the development of China's national economy; (4) potential of environmental pollution; (5) obvious inequity in

169

the agreements, contracts and articles of association signed impairing the rights and interests of one party.

F：我们是做物流生意的，而且我认为在与中方合作的时候，您刚才提到的那几种情况我们都没有涉及。那么我们需要提供什么文件供审批呢？

C：When applying for establishing a joint venture, the foreign and Chinese parties shall jointly submit the following documents to the examination and approval authority: (1) an application for the establishment of a joint venture; (2) the feasibility study report jointly prepared by the parties to the joint venture; (3) joint venture agreement, contract and articles of association signed by representatives authorized by the parties to the venture; (4) list of candidates for chairperson, vice-chairperson and directors nominated by the parties to the venture; (5) other documents required by the examination and approval authority.

F：所有这些材料都要用中文书写吗？还是可以接受英文版本的材料？

C：The documents listed in the preceding paragraph shall be written in Chinese. Documents (2), (3) and (4) may be written simultaneously in a foreign language agreed upon by the parties to the joint venture. Both versions shall have equal validity.

F：合营各方对公司所承担的责任如何分配呢？

C：A joint venture is a limited liability company. Each party to the joint venture assumes the liability of the joint venture within the limits of the capital subscribed by the party.

F：合营者以何种方式来出资呢？是仅接受货币出资呢？还是也接受其他有形或无形资产的出资？

C：Each party to a joint venture may contribute cash or buildings, factory premises, machinery, equipment or other materials, industrial property, proprietary technologies, or site use rights as investment, the value of which shall be ascertained. If the investment is in the form of buildings, factory premises, machinery, equipment or other materials, industrial property or proprietary technologies, the value shall be assessed through consultation by the parties to the joint venture on the basis of fairness and reasonableness, or shall be assessed by a third party agreed upon by parties to the joint venture.

F：那么合营企业可以在国内外开设账户以办理相关的结算和财务业务吗？
C：With a business license, a joint venture may open foreign exchange accounts and Renminbi accounts with hanks inside China. The bank handling the accounts of the joint venture shall exercise supervision of receipts and expenditures. A joint venture shall obtain permission from the State Administration of Foreign Exchange or one of its branches to open a foreign exchange deposit account with an overseas bank or one in Hong Kong or Macao, and report to the State Administration of Foreign Exchange or one of its branches its foreign exchange receipts and expenditures, and provide account balance sheets.

F：在组建合营企业后，在人事任用方面有没有相关的规定，如：高级管理职务是否一定要中方人员担任，还是外方人员也可以担任高级管理职务？
C：The general manager and deputy general managers shall be appointed by the board of directors of the joint venture. These positions may be held either by Chinese citizens or foreign citizens.

F：合营企业是否有责任支持工会？还是工会能自身解决问题？
C：A joint venture shall actively support the work of the trade union. The joint venture shall allot an amount of money totaling two percent of all salaries of the joint venture's staff and workers as trade union's funds, which the trade union of the joint venture shall use according to the relevant managerial rules for trade union funds formulated by the All China Federation of Trade Unions.

图书在版编目(CIP)数据

联络口译/王斌华,伍志伟编著.—武汉:武汉大学出版社,2010.4
(2022.1重印)
翻译资格考试必备
英语翻译核心课程系列
ISBN 978-7-307-07643-3

Ⅰ.联… Ⅱ.①王… ②伍… Ⅲ.英语—口译—教材 Ⅳ.H315.9

中国版本图书馆 CIP 数据核字(2010)第 033302 号

责任编辑:谢群英　　责任校对:刘　欣　　版式设计:马　佳

出版发行:武汉大学出版社　（430072　武昌　珞珈山）
（电子邮箱:cbs22@whu.edu.cn　网址:www.wdp.com.cn）
印刷:湖北金海印务有限公司
开本:720×1000　1/16　印张:11　字数:214 千字　插页:1
版次:2010 年 4 月第 1 版　　2022 年 1 月第 7 次印刷
ISBN 978-7-307-07643-3/H·675　　定价:30.00 元

版权所有,不得翻印;凡购我社的图书,如有质量问题,请与当地图书销售部门联系调换。